Getting Used to Weird

A very different sort of
Love Story

Lorelle Taylor

Copyright © 2019 by Lorelle Taylor
Published by Peace Angel Publishing.

All rights reserved. No part of this book may be reproduced by any mechanical, photographic, or electronic process, or in the form of a phonographic recording, nor may it be stored in a retrieval system, transmitted, or otherwise be copied for public or private use—other than for "fair use" as brief quotations embodied in articles and reviews—without prior written permission of the publisher.

ISBN 978-0-6484786-0-7 Print
ISBN 978-0-6484786-1-4 epub
ISBN 978-0-6484786-2-1 mobi

Contents

Introduction 1

The Healing 3
   The Demonstration 3
   The Course 5
   Getting Used to Weird 8
   The Psychic Reading 9

Talking to Angels and Spirit Guides 11
   Ask Your Angels 11
   Don't Worry; Be Happy 14
   Whose Messages? 16
   Talking to Dead People 17
   Mother Mary 20
   Feeling the Energy 22
   Religion Studies 22

Life Lessons: Mountain Climbing 24
   Meditation 24
   Angel Answers 25
   Buddhist Maybe Story 26
   Don't Worry; Be Happy, Again 28
   Psychic Development 28

- The Power of Now 30
- Talking to Jesus 34
- Talking to Plants and Animals 35
- I Approve of Myself 38
- Asking for Help 39

Talking to God 46
- God is Waiting 46
- Be a Light unto the World 50
- The Little Soul 52
- Factory Farmed Animals 53
- Send Your Mistakes to Heaven 56
- Friends with God 58
- Free Will is Paramount 61
- Have Faith 65
- Miracles 68
- Planning for The Future 71

Lessons of Love 74
- Love Yourself First 74
- Talk about Sex 77
- Love is All There is 80
- Love = Vibration = Healing = Sex 83
- Feeling the Love of God 86
- Ecstasy 88
- Love is Invincible 91
- Waking up with Love 92
- More Demonstrations of Love 94

- Home With God 100
  - Life and the Afterlife 100
  - Emotional Pain 102
  - 100 Virgins 103
  - Hitler 106
  - What is God? 108
  - Spiritual School 110
  - Light Being Advice 117
  - Wisdom of the Higher Self 120
  - Simultaneous and Sequential 123

- Gambling Lessons 125
  - The Test 125
  - Love for Poker Machines 131
  - Gambling Rules Your Life 132
  - The Lessons 133

- Lessons of Faith and Love 138
  - Overcoming Fear 138
  - Whose Love? 140
  - Believe and it is So 145
  - Building Confidence 147
  - Creating Your Reality 153
  - Tools for Coping 156
  - God Won't Give up on You 157
  - Be a Beacon 163
  - Avoid Violence 164

- Depression 169

- The Tools 173

The Love Story Continues.. 176

Bibliography... 181

Acknowledgments 189

Introduction

> "Our wretched species is so made that those who walk on the well-trodden path always throw stones at those who are showing a new road."
> **Voltaire (François-Marie Arouet)**

Angela wasn't like those weird ones—the ones who didn't conform and acted strangely. She was normal.

She didn't know it at the time, but now that she had joined the ranks of the weird, she realised that 'normal' people walked the well-trodden path of conformity at the expense of their *joie de vivre*. They followed what was expected of them and learned to silence their inner voices. They forgot how to interpret the feelings they received from their souls, which would lead them onto new roads, roads that were unique for every person.

Angela knew it took great courage to step onto this new road, and the temptation was always there to return to the well-trodden path. But the rewards were great and the difficulties few, so she continued down the road.

She also hoped she could encourage others to follow her,

just long enough to know they needn't take her road any more than the well-trodden path. She hoped they would find their own roads to their own great rewards, and that learning about the difficulties she had faced would help them avoid some of their own.

Angela knew that as they journeyed from normal to weird, they would also be led into love. They would become part of this very different sort of love story.

The Healing

The Demonstration

Angela knew her journey began the day she picked up that new age magazine in the supermarket. She read an article about a form of energy healing which works by awakening a frequency in the body. It sounded amazing, so she ordered a book[1].

She began practising what she learned in the book, but she wasn't sure it was real. Could she feel a slight tingling in the palms of her hands? Or was it her imagination?

Maybe she was doing something wrong. She knew she would never be convinced without a real demonstration. "Be careful what you wish for" would have been useful advice at that time.

Angela worked with her husband, Bill, in their own business, a 45 minute drive from their home in Brisbane. Bill was working at home that day, so Angela was driving herself to work when she began feeling vibration in her hands. She recognised this as the healing frequencies beginning to work, even though she hadn't said the normal intention: "Let the healing frequencies flow", as she had learned.

This time, the feeling was much stronger than she had experienced before and she felt faint. As she travelled closer to her destination, the vibration grew so strong, her hands throbbed and the fainting feeling worsened.

"I appreciate this demonstration, but can it please not happen while I'm driving?" she asked of anyone who was listening, but the feelings intensified.

Soon, Angela found herself at the back of a queue of slow moving traffic. The moment she joined the queue, the buzzing in her hands and the faint feeling doubled. She could hardly hold her head up and was in such discomfort that she couldn't sit still, but as she moved forward in the queue, the feelings grew stronger.

Then she saw it. On the side of the road was the cause of the traffic jam—an ambulance. There might have been an accident. It's possible there was a police car, but all of her energy was focused on that ambulance. As Angela approached the ambulance, it took all of her effort to stay upright in her seat. She drove with alternate hands on the steering wheel, as her hands were throbbing so much that she couldn't bear to hold on for more than a few seconds.

Angela wondered what she should do. Should she stop and make a fool of herself? Should she drive on and risk not being of help? But then she remembered what she had read in the book: one could heal from a distance. She asked the healing energy to flow into the person in the ambulance and drove on to work.

The feelings peaked as she passed the ambulance, then began to dissipate, but she had to sit in the carpark at work for a few minutes to compose herself before entering the building.

She was still trembling. She wasn't sure if it was from being frightened that she wasn't in complete control of her life, or from the awe she felt in knowing that she had just witnessed real proof that these healing frequencies existed.

The feelings may have faded, but her memories did not. As she doubted the cause of all of the other amazing, weird things that would later happen to her, she always remembered the ambulance and the effect that it initiated in her body, and she drew on that memory to bolster her faith.

The Course

After this astounding demonstration, Angela was excited to find a course she could attend to learn about how to use this amazing ability to heal.

At the course, she learned that everyone has the ability to heal themselves and to help other humans, plants, and animals heal themselves as well. She learned she could feel the powerful vibration in her hands whenever she asked the healing frequencies to flow. She didn't know it at the time, but this powerful vibration was her love, and this was her first real experience of it.

There were a lot of things Angela only became aware of with the benefit of hindsight. She later realised any healing modality could have awakened her love. She came to understand that healers simply work by awakening love within the patient. She realised this was the reason patients could heal themselves and put their bodies back into balance—love will always prevail over disease and over hatred. She now felt renewed hope as she came to realise that love could save the world.

She had been told it all along, but she had a long way to go before she would come to understand.

During the weekend of her healing course, Angela was also given an attunement procedure, designed to align the frequencies in the body. Lauren, the lady conducting the attunement, told her that sometimes the procedure allows people to understand, often for the first time, their special purpose in life.

Since her own attunement, Lauren said she was able to see spiritual beings. As she lay on the massage table and closed her eyes, Angela wondered what Lauren would see and hear, but waited until the end of the procedure to find out.

"Your special purpose in life is to be a writer. I saw two of your angels and a spirit guide named Lola. I also saw a few of your ancestors, who came to cheer you on. The angels told me that they would help you to locate your friend from school. Is there a friend that you have lost contact with?"

It had been some time since she had thought about Lynn.

Angela thought back to when she was five years old. When she and her sisters were in the yard playing cricket, they looked up to see Lynn and her younger sister standing at the fence. Their family had just moved in around the corner.

From that day on, Lynn and Angela were inseparable. They walked to school together on their first day at primary school, and continued to be best friends until Lynn moved with her family back to England, just when they started Grade 9. They lost contact with each other a few years later.

Lauren's words reminded Angela how much she had missed Lynn, and how dearly she would love to be in touch with her again.

Angela was so excited about all that happened at the course, she called her husband, Bill, to share what she learned.

"How is your witches' coven going?" Bill joked.

"This is so amazing. You can use this healing energy to heal plants and animals, yourself and other people. The lady who teaches it says she can even see the energy extending from the bodies of the patients to the hands of her students. And you should have heard Lauren, who did my attunement. She told me about my angels, and my spirit guide, and my ancestors who she saw and was talking to."

"I would have rather you kept all these details to yourself. I wish you hadn't called."

"Why?"

"This is all too weird. I'm worried you won't be 'my Angela' anymore."

"Bill, I have to be my Angela, before I can be your Angela, but I still love you."

"And I love you."

Angela cried as she hung up the phone. Angela and Bill

had lived together since Angela was 18. In their 30 years together, they had times when their relationship was strong, and others when it was strained, like most couples. But in all that time, Angela had always been able to tell Bill what she was thinking and how she was feeling. She wondered how their relationship could survive if she couldn't share these important changes in her life.

She tried to remain positive and hoped everything would work out, and in the meantime turned her attention to thoughts of being a writer.

Getting Used to Weird

Angela often considered that she might like to take up writing. Many years ago, she started writing a novel, which never progressed past a few chapters. Now that her purpose had been affirmed by Lauren, Angela started writing a book about all of the strange things happening to her.

At the healing course, she told Lauren about what happened after reading the energy healing book, when she asked for evidence that the healing frequencies were real. She had hoped for a miracle like the one she read about in the book, which described a man struggling into a healing session on crutches with a broken leg and walking out completely healed.

Instead, following a meditation session, she experienced a severe pain in her back. After lying on the floor to get some relief from the pain, she asked the healing frequencies to flow and soon began experiencing strange contorting vibrations.

What seemed like minutes, but turned out to be hours later, she heard and felt a number of clunks in her back. When she finally arose from the floor, the slight curve in her back had disappeared—her back had straightened, and her gait had changed.

"You must have found that weird," Lauren commented.

"I'm getting used to weird." Angela now knew what the name of her book was to be.

The Psychic Reading

After learning about her angels and guides appearing at her attunement, Angela was eager to learn more about them. She made an appointment for her first ever tarot reading with an intuitive consultant named Teresa.

When she met Teresa, Angela immediately released the trepidation she had felt at the thought of where this tide was taking her.

"Where do you think this information is coming from?" Angela asked during the reading.

Teresa had such a peaceful, loving, manner, that Angela easily believed her when she answered: "From the divine."

Her tarot reading gave her a deeper understanding of her life's path, and a few pointers on how to proceed. She didn't know where this path was leading her, but she knew it was her love that was guiding her.

"You signed a new soul contract about five months ago," Teresa told her.

"Funny, I don't remember that, but it might explain all

of the weird things that I have been experiencing lately."

Teresa confirmed what Lauren had told her: "You have angels and spirit guides who wish to communicate with you."

Angela thought it was time to find out more about them.

Talking to Angels and Spirit Guides

Ask Your Angels

During the reading, Teresa told Angela to read the books she had at home on her bookshelf. Angela had bought them years earlier, and one addressed communication with angels. *Ask Your Angels* by Alma Daniel, Timothy Wyllie and Andrew Ramer[2], detailed elaborate exercises that taught Angela how to raise her vibration closer to the higher vibration of the angelic realm.

The book guided her through the GRACE process: Grounding, Releasing, Alignment, Conversing, and Enjoyment. Although they took some patience, she gradually worked through most of the exercises. Patience had never been one of Angela's strong points, but her perseverance paid off.

After performing a grounding meditation, releasing her feelings of fear and unworthiness, and aligning with the angels' higher vibration through a visualisation exercise, she was ready to converse with her angels. Enjoyment came slowly as her confidence increased.

Her angels introduced themselves as Abno and Abow. Angela was told that Abno was her guardian angel and Abow was an angel of transition, who was with her to help her move on with her new life. Abno told her that the name Angela meant Messenger and was derived from the word angel. She already knew this, but it took on greater significance, now that she talked with angels.

She couldn't see the angels—only hear them. It wasn't like someone was speaking into her ear, but directly into her brain. With hindsight, she realised how crazy this sounded, but at the time it made perfect sense. After all, it was what the book told her could happen.

She didn't need the book to tell her it was real. There were so many messages of love, of the love the angels had for her, and of the love dwelling within her. There were many messages which she didn't really understand: she was surrounded by love, and she could just breathe it in; she could be a beacon of love and light for all the world.

> Abno: *Before you begin to believe, you must first have faith. Then you will become one with the angels. If you first believe in yourself, you will become a better listener and will be among the angels. The purpose of the new world order is that you will become one with the angels. Believe me when I say you are among the lucky ones who will be a voice for love and peace.*

As she received the messages, she wrote them directly into her notebook. This way, she could write what was said without filtering the information through her logical mind, which could insert words into their conversation, if she wasn't careful.

Before joining Bill in the business, Angela spent 13 years working for the Australian Government in the Social Security department. There, she developed the abilities to listen attentively to clients, and to write quickly as she took their statements. She realised that these skills were helping her now.

However, sometimes Angela was amazed at the words she wrote and thought there must be a mistake, only to find later that it all made sense:

Abno: *There is much to be done, but with our help you will be able to achieve all of your goals. Love will prevail. Love is like a hot poker.*

Angela: I don't think that's right.

Abno: *Love is like a beautiful dove. It flies out and poops on people.*

Angela: That can't be right, can it?

Abno: *You are a child of God and love is always present in your life. You can be your very best person and love will prevail.*

Your love is like a beautiful flower and you are its petals. Your love is your connection to the creator and your guides. Your love is your best weapon against hatred and racism.

Your love is your best weapon against the troubles in your life and others lives. Your love is your link to the universe.

You can be whatever you want to be. You can be your true self and know that love will prevail. You can sit on the fence and be a pawn, or you can become your own person and be a voice for love and truth.

You are one with the universe and love will prevail. Let love be your guide and take a leap of faith in the journey of your life. Be at one with the world and its people. Be at one with the love of God. Be at peace.

Your love is like a hot poker. It is forever glowing and alive.

Don't Worry; Be Happy

She applied the same techniques when communicating with her spirit guides, and she learned that different spirit guides helped her with different aspects of her life. Lola told Angela that her area of expertise was Angela's spiritual development and offered profound messages, some of which only made sense years later.

Lola: *You should know that your life is a series of lessons, and the lessons need not be unpleasant, as some of your previous ones have been.*

Angela: That's good to know.

Lola: *Your life is all too short and you can know that there is much to be done, but you should also know that life is meant to be enjoyed. So you should try to make the most of each day, each minute. Don't worry about what lies ahead. We are all here to help you. Have faith. Have courage. Have love. Your life will be a model for others to follow, so you should consider whatever you do and how it will affect others. It is a big responsibility, but know that you are not alone and you have help now and always. Don't worry. Be happy.*

Angela: Lola, I am concerned I may make an incorrect decision because my intuition is not so finely developed. Is there anything I should know about that?

Lola: *Choose the path that feels right to you at the time, and you will know if you step from the path, as your feelings will tell you. Have faith in your abilities. Have faith in yourself. Have faith in us. Love will prevail. Don't worry. Be happy. Be forever in love. Be at peace.*

Angela didn't quite understand why Lola was telling her that people would look to her to be an example for them. She guessed that anyone in the public eye could be seen as an example others may wish to emulate, like movie stars and prominent sportsmen and women who understand this responsibility. She thought this sounded like good news for the success of her book, but she wondered if such a responsibility may become a burden. But then she realised that everyone is a role model for someone—for their children, employees, siblings, and friends. Angela decided she should take the advice that was offered and not worry, but be happy. That was the example she could set.

This was a common theme to the messages from her guides and angels.

> Abno: *Be aware of the love around you every day. You will know the right thing to do when you feel joy in your decisions. Joy will accompany you wherever you go. Love is the key. Love yourself and all you come in contact with and you will be alright. Don't worry. Be happy.*

Whose Messages?

The angelic communications were not always without difficulties. She later learned that some of the messages which she thought had come from her angels had really come from her own mind, when the information she thought they gave her had turned out to be false.

Angela awoke one night in the middle of the night and was unable to sleep. After a day of experiencing anger and frustration, she asked if angels have emotions, and received this answer:

Angels are from the light. The light is love. Love is an emotion. Angels have emotion, but it is always love.

Angela considered these words an indication of where the communication might be coming from. A message from an angel may not always be what she wanted to hear, but it was always delivered with love.

Talking to Dead People

There were many times during her communications with the spirit realm and their aftermath when Angela doubted her sanity. Her sanity became more questionable, however, when she began communicating with deceased loved ones.

Angela and her eldest sister, Vera, attended a seminar conducted by John Edward, the world famous psychic medium. Angela had asked Vera along as the family genealogy expert and if any of their distant relatives came through, Vera would know who they were. Vera wasn't really a believer, but she had an open mind.

They were driving out of the car park, feeling very disappointed that they didn't get a reading at the seminar, when on the car radio they played the song: "Sisters are Doing it For Themselves". Angela wondered if this could be a message. She received her answer, not ten minutes later, when the same radio station played the same song again: "Sisters are Doing it For Themselves".

"Hey! They just played that song a minute ago."

"Really?" Vera did not notice the song or its significance.

"Well, maybe that's why we didn't get a reading; we sisters are supposed to do it for ourselves."

Brought up in a Christian family, Angela had reservations

about talking to people from the other side. These reservations could have easily turned to fear after watching *The Exorcism of Emily Rose* on TV. She started to wonder if she might end up like Emily Rose, or Reagan in *The Exorcist*. Although she hadn't experienced any head swivelling or green vomit, she was happy to learn from her spiritual helpers that the negative energies portrayed in these movies were greatly overdramatised, and prayers of protection could put her mind at rest.

Angela bought books on the subject and purchased a set of CDs recorded by John Edward[3], which included lessons and meditations designed to develop psychic abilities. She knew, too, that she always had the help of her angels and guides.

> Angela: Lola, in regards to my talking to people who have crossed over, like my friend, Karen, who I spoke to yesterday, I would like some information about how that works. In John Edward's book[4], he said he raises his vibration through prayer and meditation in order to get the messages that he gets. How can I just hear Karen without any major preparation? And what will everyone who reads my book need to do?
>
> Lola: *Hello, Angela. You can know that you are able to hear the voice of a loved one much more easily than the voice of a stranger. There is a constant connection between you and those that you love. Communicating with a loved one is much easier for most people. Communicating with strangers can take a little more work. Do not be afraid to*

tell people in your book that they can easily communicate with their loved ones. Ask and you shall receive. Love is the key.

She certainly loved her parents, and her friend, Karen, who had died suddenly a few years earlier. Angela was happy to receive messages from them, until they asked her to convey messages to those still living.

When she plucked up the courage to come out of the closet and relay the messages, not all of the messages were cheerfully accepted. Occasionally, some of the messages also contained incorrect information and Angela never knew if she made a mistake in transcribing the messages or she had been given the wrong details. She did not think she was mentally unstable as some of her family had implied. Again, with hindsight, she could finally consider the possibility that mistakes were all part of the divine plan to prepare her family for the future when her questionable sanity would become an advantage.

She was able to understand why her husband, Bill, and her middle sister, Gail, in particular, had trouble hearing the messages she tried to convey to them. Even though Angela had seen evidence of reincarnation and spirit communication in the Bible, she knew that Gail was staunchly religious, and her religious faith didn't allow for a belief in the ability to talk to deceased loved ones. Angela knew that Bill was just as staunchly atheistic, and his perspective didn't allow for a belief in much at all. However, that understanding didn't make their reaction any less painful for Angela.

She was also upset and embarrassed about the incorrect messages, but she always knew, deep in her heart, that these messages were not all coming from her unhinged mind.

Mother Mary

One day, whilst meditating, Angela heard the words "Virgin Mary". After asking to speak only to guides of the highest vibration as usual, she asked the following:

> Angela: Mother Mary (mother of Jesus), if you are here, I would love to hear from you.
>
> Mother Mary: *Yes, Angela, I am here. I have come to tell you about your work with the animals. You can know that...*
>
> Angela: I am sorry, Mary. I am not doing very well with this.
>
> Mother Mary: *You are doing fine, Angela. Just relax and listen.*
>
> Angela: Ok.
>
> Mother Mary: *You can know that I am here to help you with your work in looking after the animals. I have many things I can help you with, including being a voice for women in the world. You are concerned about the plight*

of women in your society and in other societies around the world, specifically in Islamic societies. Do not fear. There are many here who can help you. Be not afraid. All will be well. Call on me when you need some assistance in your work with animals and women's rights. We can work together to help both of these for better lives.

Angela: Thanks, Mary. It is an honour to have you visit me.

Mother Mary: *I, too, am honoured to talk to you. You are doing a wonderful job. Do not fear. All will be well.*

Angela: Thank you, Mary.

Mother Mary: *Go now and send your love out into the world and multiply your love tenfold.*

Angela: Thank you, Mother Mary.

Mother Mary: *You are welcome, Angela. You can help to send the message to the world, that love needs to become paramount in people's lives. You can be a beacon of love and light, and remind them that they are made of love, and all can be a beacon. All can have an effect on improving the state of affairs for all the people of the Earth, and the Earth herself. You can do much to help the situation, and indeed you are, by sending your love out into the world every day. Go now and be a beacon of love and light for the world. Be at peace.*

Feeling the Energy

Angela had read in Sonia Choquette's book, *Ask Your Guides*[5], the suggestion of greeting each spiritual entity or group of entities each morning, and taking this time to identify their energies. In her early days of talking to angels and spirit guides, she had tried this and had some success.

Some days, she said, "Good morning, Archangels," and could feel their loving but powerful energy. When she said, "Good morning, Ministry of Angels," she felt their light energy, like being surrounded by butterflies. Saying "Good morning, Abno," she felt the loving light of her guardian angel. "Good morning, Lola," was responded with a loving, but serious energy that reminded her of a school ma'am. On those days, she could also easily discern the distinctive energies of her mum, her dad, and her friend, Karen.

Then there were other days, when she just drew a blank.

But the day she spoke with Mother Mary, she knew exactly what it was like to feel another being's energy. Mother Mary had an energy as smooth as silk. It felt like the shawl, which Mary was so often depicted wearing, was wrapped lovingly around Angela's shoulders. She had no doubts that this conversation was real.

Religion Studies

About ten years earlier, Angela was reading through the Open Learning University subject lists. She had seen there were language classes on TV and considered learning

Japanese. The next thing Angela knew, she was enrolling in religion studies, a comparative study of the world's major religions—Judaism, Christianity, Islam, Hinduism and Buddhism.

She told others she wanted to find out about the real story of Islam, after all the bad publicity it received in the Australian media. Although this was true, it wasn't her full story. She felt a compulsion to undertake this study; a strong, and totally inexplicable compulsion.

From applying to completing the course, Angela had the feeling that it was not only her will keeping her so committed. She seemed to have an extra willpower that felt like it came from outside herself. After she passed the exam, that feeling just disappeared.

Although her extra willpower left her, the knowledge that she gained from the course did not. The main thing she learned from the course was the common ground that she found in each of the faiths. Each one had a version of the Golden Rule: "Do unto others, as you would have them do unto you".

It was only later that she would learn of the significance of this knowledge.

Life Lessons: Mountain Climbing

Meditation

Angela began to meditate regularly. She discovered the Meditation Society of Australia's website[6] and downloaded lessons and meditations. She learned of many methods from many sources. Some were designed to allow deep relaxation, and some seemed more useful in helping her raise her vibration to talk to the spirit realm.

After raising her vibration during meditation, she would talk to her angels and spirit guides, and she began to look forward to their regular conversations. Whenever life caused her confusion or pain, her angels and guides were there to help her. They couldn't make the pain go away, but they helped her put it in perspective. They told her that even her painful times could be cherished, if she looked at them with love.

She never quite understood this, but she had plenty of times to put it into practice. Angela and Bill's business caused them stress and worry, and someone took out a lawsuit against them, which took the stress levels completely off the scale. But it was the deeper life lessons that caused her the most pain.

She could not explain the pain to anyone in a way they would understand. She was learning how to have faith in the universe to bring her her desires. She was learning to have faith in God to be all love, and to be a confident, faithful, invincible beacon of God's love. She was learning to have faith in herself and her creative abilities. The pain came when she thought she failed at all of these lessons. Over time, she realised the journey was just as important as the achievements.

To help her with her life lessons, there were many resources she discovered. She found books about living in the moment, about the law of attraction, and about communicating with God. She learned about other healing modalities, and she learned about tarot.

Angel Answers

Angela found inspiration from many sources, including the book, *Angel Messages From the Beyond: The Complete Book of Answers*, by Juan Nakamori[7], which contains 82 angel messages. As she calmed her mind and thought of a question, the answer came by way of a number between 1 and 82. Her question was always a general "Is there anything I need to know right now?" and the answer nearly every time was 11. It became a running joke between Angela and the angels. Number 11 came up first, then followed by number 22. She guessed these were messages she really needed to learn.

11[7]

There is nothing in this world that is not worth
Cherishing.
Beautiful things, ugly things, petty things,
New things, outdated things,
Praise that feels pleasant to the ear,
Good news, health or illness,
Hard work, the kind-hearted, and even the egotistical:
All are to be cherished…
If you observe calmly from a broader perspective,
You will begin to see all things differently.
True meaning—that which has been hidden until now
Will then be revealed to you.
Because, when you see through the mind's eye of
your True Self,
Whatever is no longer necessary for you
Will no longer bother you,
And will disappear from your sight.
Through cherishing the people things and situations
in your life,
You cherish and nurture your True Self.

Buddhist Maybe Story

It was during a visit with some friends at the Buddhist retreat, Chenrezig in Eudlo, Queensland, when Angela heard a story illustrating the concept of cherishing every occurrence in our lives.

The Buddhist nun told the story of an old farmer:

The farmer's only horse ran away. The neighbours came to commiserate, because they knew the farmer would not be able to plough.

"What bad luck," they said.

"Maybe," said the farmer.

The next day the horse returned and brought with it six wild horses.

"Your bad luck has become good luck," congratulated the neighbours.

"Maybe," the farmer replied.

The following day the farmer's son tried to ride one of the wild horses and fell and broke his leg. The neighbours came to offer their sympathy.

"Your son won't be able to help you on the farm. How can you possibly handle all the work on your own? This is truly a disaster for you."

"Maybe," was the reply.

The day afterwards, the army came to conscript all of the young men from the village. Because of his broken leg, the farmer's son was rejected.

When the neighbours came again, they said, "Many young men die in the war, and your son could have been one of them. You are lucky after all."

And the old farmer said, "Maybe."

Don't Worry; Be Happy, Again

To Angela, this story also reinforced the message her angels and spirit guides told her. It was also the basis for the second of the messages from the Angel Messages book: "Don't worry. Be happy."

> 22[7]
> Humour is a kind of magic…
> As you become able to observe things
> With a relaxed mind and humour,
> You will also be able to laugh off the hard things
> And transform them into sources of power.

Psychic Development

Angela enrolled in a weekly psychic development course. Her teacher, Jayne, taught that everyone has psychic abilities. She also believed that by the time most people approach the age of 50, as Angela was, they were more likely to have forgotten how to use these abilities, if they had been ignored. An enthusiastic student, Angela absorbed the lessons about chakras, auras, how to do flower readings, and psychometry. Her favourite part of the course, however, was divination card reading.

Angela began collecting cards. She had cards with messages from angels, ascended masters, dragonfae, animal spirits, and even Wiccan spells. She also found some tarot cards among her things, purchased twenty years earlier. She loved the feeling which all her cards gave her—that she was beginning to awaken her long-forgotten intuition.

When Jayne offered a two-weekend course in tarot reading, Angela was keen to attend. Bill, however, was against the idea. Since Angela's healing course, the witches' coven, as he called it, it was clear he didn't believe in anything Angela believed in—not God, not the afterlife, not angels—nothing. He tolerated her interest in these things, as long as she kept them completely to herself. He didn't want to discuss them, and he certainly didn't want them affecting him. Bill had accepted her talking to angels and guides, probably because he thought she was really talking to herself. Tarot reading, however, was just too weird for him.

"It's not like talking to angels. It seems more like witchcraft to me."

Angela knew that it was more than a coincidence that the tarot cards she had bought so many years ago were called *Angel Tarot*. She showed him the box, and began to pray that Bill would come to not only accept her beliefs, but also share them. She eventually talked him into letting her attend the tarot course. It was a start.

Jayne's class was based on the Rider-Waite cards, but Angela also purchased other tarot cards which spoke to her more personally. She slowly learned the meaning of all the cards, and learned that she would have a new spirit guide to help her with the tarot. Jayne suggested that she only communicate with one spirit guide now, or she would become too confused, so she conversed only with Allan, her new guide.

The Power of Now

As well as helping with her tarot readings, Angela was very grateful to have Allan's help with many of her life lessons.

The stresses of everyday life and work were starting to get her down again. Often the stress related to money. As designers and manufacturers of electronic equipment, the business needed to stay at the forefront of technological advances. Components that were bought in the expectation of major sales one year became obsolete junk the next. Juggling finances was always a concern.

Angela was beginning to feel like a failure because she wasn't able to live in the moment, as she learned about from the book, *The Power of Now* by Eckhart Tolle[8]. This feeling of failing not only made her depressed, but she felt grumpier and grumpier. While she tried to embrace her new knowledge, her work included following the exchange rates and choosing the best time to pay foreign currency bills. She couldn't see how to do this job and live completely in the present moment, so she became angry instead. Unconscious of what was happening for her, she was drowning in her emotions and wondering how to get out of the pool.

> Allan: *Angela, you can know that all will be well. You can have faith in your abilities. You are doing better than you think. Even though you are becoming angry at times, you are becoming aware of this, and your awareness is a major step towards releasing this emotion.*

Angela: How can I stop becoming angry?

Allan: *If you can live in the now, as your book explains, you can go a long way towards not needing anger. Your anger, as you have deduced, is a form of fear. Living in the now eliminates fear. There is nothing to fear in your present moment, ever. The other thing you can do is to think love for yourself and all involved in the situation.*

Angela: It is hard to think love and live in the now when I am so caught up in my fear. When my job is to think about the future—whether the exchange rate will go up or down—I have no choice but to think about the future. I understand about living in the now. I just find it difficult to do it in difficult circumstances—well, in most circumstances, actually.

Allan: *Angela, you do not give yourself enough credit. You have done very well. You are right; it is hard in difficult circumstances. But difficulties are only difficulties because you perceive them so. As for how you remain focused on the present when your job calls for you to think about the future, you can know that you must think of the future from your position in the present. You can know that in the present moment, you will make the best decision possible.*

Angela: How can this be? In relation to the exchange rates for instance, if I fail to buy at the best exchange rate, it will cost our company a lot of money.

Allan: *Yes, but remember the universe is always looking out for you. What you lose on the roundabouts, you will gain on the swings, so to speak. Do not fear for tomorrow. Let tomorrow take care of itself. The universe will see you right. Your love will see you through any difficulties. Have faith. Have love. Do not fear. There is nothing to fear in this world or the next.*

Angela: But if I don't do things right, as far as what the exchange rate will do, I will be seen to be negligent in my duties, as I was on Wednesday.

Allan: *Bill helped you with that and all was well. The universe is helping you, including all the people of the Earth. Sometimes they just don't realise it. Everyone is helping each other, whether consciously or unconsciously. Have no fear. You cannot fail.*

Angela: This is another giant leap of faith.

Allan: *Yes, Angela, faith in the law of attraction and the universe's ability to provide all of your needs and desires is required. But once you have faith, it is no longer needed, because the results will be obvious to all.*

Angela: I understand. Thanks, Allan. Thanks so much for all your help. I really appreciate it.

On that previous Wednesday, Angela decided to hold off paying a large invoice hoping to see a more favourable exchange rate in the following few days. When Bill learned of this, he insisted on paying the invoice at the bad exchange rate that day rather than paying it at a disastrous rate in a few days' time. They paid the bill that day, only to see the exchange rate worsen in the next few days. Bill was right and it made Angela question her own judgement.

During the pressures of work, Angela had many opportunities to practise living in the now. She had difficulty replacing their receptionist who recently resigned. As Angela filled in on reception, she found the constant activity particularly stressful. Although she longed for the time when she would be relieved of reception duties, she tried to focus on the job at hand and appreciate the chance it gave her to practise what she had learned.

When she did find a replacement receptionist, her first week held stresses of its own, while keeping up with the workflow and the training process. Angela's busy schedule caused her to miss a few days of meditation, and she suffered from real stress. When she finally found the time for meditation and asked to speak to high vibrational guides, Allan offered helpful advice, as usual:

> Allan: *As you are now aware, if you miss your meditation, the stresses of the world begin to accumulate in your body and in your mind. Your meditation allows you to release all of these stresses, and allows you to cope better with new stresses that come along. But as you learned, if you can live in the moment, you need not stress.*

Stress is really just worry about the future. Remember that the future will take care of itself. Live for the moment. Yes, you can plan for the future, but from a position in the present. These are difficult concepts to grasp, but once you have grasped them, you need never stress about the future again. Think love in all situations and all will be well. Your love will see you through. Have some fun. Laughter is the best medicine. Love and peace go with you. Be at peace.

Talking to Jesus

It became a habit for Angela to do a tarot reading for herself every day. One tarot card with which she became very familiar was the Eight of Cups. Her version of the card depicted a man just starting to ascend a large craggy mountain. Angela came to dread this card, as it always appeared when she had another mountain to climb, another life lesson to overcome.

Both Abno and Allan told her she need have no fear, and eventually even Jesus did, as well.

Jesus came to her one night during her meditation, in which she was learning to raise her vibration using one of John Edward's psychic development CDs[3]. Jesus became a regular visitor, and during the many conversations that followed, he taught her how to raise her vibration without any outside assistance. In the early days, however, she came to know when Jesus wanted to talk to her by the particular sensation of the increased vibration she felt.

During his first visit, Jesus allowed Angela to feel his distinctive energy, which she described as being sweet and loving. Although she felt unworthy of his love, Jesus allowed her to feel it regularly. He told her that he was always available to Angela, and anyone who calls on him, to help with life lessons or healing.

After her initial conversation with Jesus, Angela remembered that she had bought a book many years ago, called *I Am With You Always: True Stories of Encounters With Jesus* by G. Scott Sparrow, Ed.D.[9], which related stories of other people who had been helped by Jesus. Others had been frightened to tell their stories, for fear of being called crazy, so the book allowed them to remain anonymous. Angela wondered what people would think of her.

She knew they would call her crazy. But she didn't feel crazy. She felt as though she had this ability her whole life, and felt rather betrayed by her society which had discouraged its development.

Her conversation with Jesus left her feeling honoured, replacing her initial feeling of surprise.

There were, of course, many more surprises to come.

Talking to Plants and Animals

Angela and Bill had booked a cruise of the South Pacific, even though they had to borrow money against their house to do it. Bill was suffering from depression, so Angela saw the cruise as a good investment and hoped it would help him overcome his condition.

As they were preparing to go, Angela wanted to find a place outside to hang her orchid, where it would get rain. She decided on a branch of a lemon tree in their front garden, and for some reason, she decided she should ask the tree for permission, before taking the liberty of hanging a heavy plant from its branch. To her surprise, she received an indignant reply: "No, it is *not* ok!"

She hadn't expected to receive any reply, let alone such a vehement one. Angela was tempted to ignore it, thinking that it surely must be her imagination, but, just in case, she moved her orchid to another tree, and when she asked it the same question, was told: "Yes. It's ok."

Another time, she was walking through a field, when she noticed a few dragonflies following her about. They would stop when she stopped, and move when she moved. She asked the one that stopped closest to her "What are you doing?"

She thought she received a reply: "Minding."

"Minding what?" Angela asked.

"Minding you," was the response.

Could it be, she wondered, that we can really communicate with plants, animals and insects? Is it possible that we have had this ability all along, but we forgot how to listen? She knew what some people would think: that she just made up these answers. But then she had tried to communicate with other creatures, and not heard any reply whatsoever. Surely if she made up responses on one occasion, she would do it every time.

Angela wanted to let people know that this sort of

communication was possible for everyone, so she was pleased to have this confirmed later by God. For the moment, however, she was happy that Jesus answered her question about dragonflies.

Angela: Jesus, can you tell me the role of the dragonfly?

Jesus: *Yes, Angela. The fairies have asked the dragonflies to look out for you. They appreciate the help you have given to them for the environment and animals, and wish to try to repay you. The dragonflies are there to remind you of their love and caring. You can call on the fairies to help with any of your work with the environment or animals. The dragonflies can help to lift your spirits, and can provide practical assistance in the outdoors with directions, etc.*

Angela: I appreciate all this help. Thank you, fairies and dragonflies. Thanks, Jesus for the explanation. Were there any other messages?

Jesus: *Angela, you can be a beacon in your darkest hour. Your light shines out as a shining example to others in times of stress. Your love sheds light on the darkness. You are a beacon of light and love. Please send your light and love out into the world. Don't forget to love yourself first. Be at peace.*

I Approve of Myself

Although Angela learned that she should love herself, she was not certain how to achieve this.

When reading *You Can Heal Your Life* by Louise Hay[10], she found an answer . Repeating the affirmation, "I approve of myself", for some inexplicable reason, left her feeling happy again. Angela realised she needed to forgive herself for being imperfect, and that she was blaming others for the same failing. After repeating, "I approve of myself", she was able to do just that.

The next day during her meditation, when she asked to speak to high vibrational guides, Jesus came to her.

> Angela: Hello, Jesus. Is that you?
>
> Jesus: *Yes, Angela, it is I. It is good that you recognise my energy.*
>
> Angela: I wasn't entirely sure.
>
> Jesus: *I know, but your perception is improving. I am here to let you know what a good job you are doing in living in the moment, and loving yourself and the world. Your affirmation of "I approve of myself" is working well.*
>
> Angela: Yes. I don't quite understand why, but it makes me feel good.
>
> Jesus: *It works by releasing the negativity you have built up in relation to yourself. You can know that all will be*

well. You are doing an excellent job. Just remember to love yourself before you send your love out into the world. Remember that love is the key to success in all things.

Your love is like a diamond. It sends light out in all directions. One source of light becomes many.

Remember that your love will see you through any difficulties. Do not fear.

Have faith in yourself and your abilities. Have faith in the universe and its ability to bring you all that you desire. Think love in all that you do, and you can't go wrong. Your love is the key to success in all you do.

Take heart. Take love. Take mine.

Be of good cheer. Your love can go a long way towards solving the problems you encounter, both in your personal life, in your business life, and in the world. But remember that everyone in the world has free will to accept or reject your advice, and to accept or reject your love, your healing, your peace.

Have faith, have love, and all will be well. Don't worry. Be happy. Love will see you through. Be at peace.

Asking for Help

Jesus came to Angela often, to help with her lessons. As the lessons unfolded, she didn't realise how important they were becoming to her. She was only aware when she failed in applying them, or when she succeeded. It seemed that each time she succeeded in conquering another lesson, there was another mountain to climb, right behind the last one, just as her dreaded tarot card predicted.

One of those mountains related to staying positive about the court case. The judge had dismissed the case, but the plaintiff had appealed the decision. It was a long, stressful three months till Angela and Bill heard that the appeals court decided in their favour. They wept in each other's arms as they released three years of stress and tension.

"If we cry so much over a win, I hate to think what we'd be like if we lost," Angela laughed, as the tears spilled onto Bill's shoulder.

While one problem was behind them, the court case had caused their business to haemorrhage money while it also kept Angela and Bill busy with affidavits, solicitor's meetings, and paperwork. Just when it looked like they might be able to devote more time to their business, the global financial crisis hit with a fresh set of difficulties.

Angela turned to Jesus for help.

> Jesus: *You cannot change one thing about the morrow by worrying about it. Action in your present moment can change your morrow, but thinking and worrying about it will not.*
>
> *But you need to be centred in your present moment first. In your present moment, you can be conscious of what that present moment holds for you, and then go on to plan a*

course of action in relation to tomorrow, whilst always coming back to the present moment. Breathe in the present moment. Concentrate on the present moment, and the means of tackling the perceived difficulties of the morrow will become more apparent. If you ask for it, you can get help with all these things. Ask and you shall receive.

Angela: Can I not just ask for a blanket help for everything I do?

Jesus: *Yes, Angela. But remember that you need be careful what you ask for—for you may just get it. You may get help in a way that you do not appreciate, if you ask for blanket help on everything. Also, you came forth into this physical world with goals that you wanted to achieve, things that you wanted to do. You really don't want help with everything, because then it would not be your achievement, but others.*

Angela: Why do we all not have a better idea of all of our goals and our soul's desires?

Jesus: *If you came into the world with a list planted in your brain of those things you wanted to get done, you may miss the beauty and the lessons along the way. Your higher self reveals your goals to you one at a time, and you have all the help that you need and desire, to achieve those goals. But they are your goals that you need to achieve on your own behalf. You can get help, but there are certain parts of your life that you need to do yourself. It is your life. We can provide help, the universe can provide help, but you are the one in the driver's seat, so to speak. We can point you in the right direction, let you know when you have strayed off the path, but you need to drive there yourself. Do you understand?*

Angela: I think so. Thanks, Jesus. How will I know which achievements I can get help with, and which I can do on my own?

Jesus: *Meditation is the key to being in touch with your higher self. During meditation, you come to know what is right for you as a physical being. Start your meditation with a question about which you want your higher self's view, and the answer will come during meditation.*

But do not fear, Angela. There are many things that you can receive help with, and the universe is here to see that you and everyone else achieve their desires.

Angela knew that their business was one thing she wanted to ask for help with. They were barely managing to pay their bills and staff each month, and nothing they did seemed to help. It had been a long time since Angela had spoken to her guardian angel, Abno, and she wondered if there was anything Abno could do to help them.

Angela: Can you please help me to find a way to get out of debt quickly—for both our business and ourselves.

Abno: *Angela, you need to accept the situation as you find it, before you can change it. Accept your indebtedness as part of your life. Embrace that part of your life and cherish it. There are lessons there for you, as in all parts of your life. Once you have accepted your life as it is, it will begin to change automatically.*

Angela: How does one accept being in debt?

Abno: *One must believe in the power of the universe to relieve you of your debt and to create the kind of reality one desires. You need to believe in your own creative abilities also. But first, love the life you have now. The indebtedness is worth cherishing, just as much as any other condition you find yourself in.*

Angela: I sort of understand that. Are you saying that I can love my life no matter what? I would prefer things to be different, but the way that things are now is acceptable and loveable. Because no matter what condition my life is in, I am always connected to God. I always have your help and the help of my guides. And quite frankly, I am invincible no matter what happens to me. Is that what you are saying?

Abno: *Yes Angela. That is exactly what I am saying. Well done.*

Angela: Thanks, Abno. Bye for now.

Abno: *I am always here if you need me, Angela. Call on me at anytime.*

Although Angela started to accept their indebtedness, they had to consider putting off staff in order to allow their business to survive. Angela asked Jesus for help with this decision.

> Jesus: *Angela, what answer do you get when you ask, "What would love do now?"*
>
> Angela: I get the answer that the business needs to survive for the good of the all.
>
> Jesus: *Then this is your answer. Your first thought when asking "What would love do now?" This is the answer to your question. Love is the answer to every question, and God has given each of us the ability to judge what love would do. Have faith in your decision-making abilities. Have faith in Bill's as well. You are all doing the best that you can in any situation, and remember that love will always prevail.*
>
> *Think love before taking any action, and it is sure to be loving action that you take. Think love before any thought, and your thoughts will be loving thoughts.*
>
> *Angela, you can know that you are doing a wonderful job of living in the moment. Have faith in yourself. Have faith in your creative abilities. Have faith in the universe. Remember that God has put in place the perfect system to allow you to achieve your goals, whilst all others achieve theirs as well. Have faith in the system and all will be well.*

Angela was very grateful for the help she received from Jesus, and her guides and angels, but she knew that God was her greatest source of help.

Talking to God

God is Waiting

She had read that it was possible to talk to God—to have a two-way conversation with him, but for a long time, she didn't have the courage to try. She knew that she would be obliged to tell the world what God had to say, and she was frightened by that responsibility. She knew that some people would say she was blaspheming to claim to have spoken to Jesus, but if she claimed to talk to God, the number of such people would multiply.

Yet, she finally plucked up the courage. With the help of a book by Michelle Epiphany Prosser, *Excuse Me, Your God is Waiting*[11], she overcame fear and feelings of unworthiness, and finally spoke to God.

> Angela: God, are you there?
>
> God: *Yes, Angela, I am here.*
>
> Angela: I don't have any questions. I just wanted to know if I could hear your voice.

God: *You can hear my voice, if you listen with all your heart, with all your soul, with all your mind, and with all your ears.*

Angela: Is your voice the same as Jesus' voice?

God: *No. Jesus speaks to you as an individual, who is undoubtedly part of the all. I speak on behalf of all creation as you know it.*

Angela: Should I be writing this down?

God: *Yes, Angela, you should.*

Angela: I felt a great responsibility writing down the words I believed that Jesus was speaking to me. Writing the words that I believe God is speaking to me seems to increase the responsibility exponentially.

God: *Yes, Angela, it is a big responsibility, but you are up to the task. Relax. I am always with you, just as Jesus is. I am not going anywhere. When you feel more confident in your abilities, more sure of your responsibility, you can speak to me again.*

In the meantime, know that I will never let you down. I am always here to provide for you, just as I do for the sparrow in the Bible. Ask and you shall receive. But know that when you came into this world, you had certain goals that you wanted to achieve. You would not be fulfilled if you allowed someone else to achieve those goals on your behalf. Have fun with your life. Strive to do those things which you came here to do, but remember that help is always available to you.

Be at peace. Go and have some fun. Don't forget to love yourself in all that you do.

Angela: Thank you, God. I love you.

God: *And I, you.*

The quote from Abraham in the Abraham-Hicks newsletter 7th October 2008[12], read:

> "When that which is God—or that which is that which man calls "God"—is being understood by man, man has to translate it into the format he understands. But this Energy—this Source that man is giving the label of "God", cannot be quantified in any thing that man understands. And as man attempts to do it, the distortions are enormous."

Deepak Chopra's book, *How To Know God*[13], explained that God is different things to different people. Angela came to think that the one true God is such a flexible thing, that he/she can be whatever we need him/her to be, which means that all religions probably contain truth about God, and all religions probably contain distortions as well. One thing she felt certain about was that the first thing she learned in Sunday School was probably true. God is love.

Angela's father had been a Congregational Church minister prior to Angela's birth, but was forced to resign the ministry and get a better paid job to feed his wife and daughters, Vera, Gail, and Elizabeth (Beth). Religion wasn't forced down their throats at home, but the children attended Sunday School and church until they went to high school.

Although Angela had been raised as a Christian, she made up her own mind about what to believe in. She didn't believe in the God of wrath of the Old Testament, preferring to look to Jesus in the Gospels for his example of the life she should be aspiring to.

She had a belief in God for most of her life, but it was when she was learning about biology at school, that Angela came to have complete faith that there was a God. She learned about the interconnection of all life on Earth—how the trees transpire water from their leaves, which evaporates along with the water from the ocean, then wafts as clouds, and falls again for us to drink; the way the trees inhale the carbon dioxide that we exhale, and provide us with the oxygen we need to live. There were many such examples which gave Angela confidence in a creator of this complete system.

Although her society accepted a belief in God and Jesus, these topics were not discussed in a public forum. Even though she had been raised a Christian, it was rare for Angela to experience discussions about an individual's love for God and Jesus, so she felt great fear in declaring her love to the world in her book.

At the beginning of her next meditation, Angela apologised

to God and Jesus, for allowing fear to get in the way of her love for them. During the meditation, Jesus came to respond.

> Jesus: *Do not fear. You will never be required to do more than you are happy with. I know that you were concerned when typing your book, that you would be putting yourself out on a limb, when it comes to declaring your love for myself and God. But remember that we are here to support that limb. God will never let you down.*
>
> *Trust in the Lord. Trust in the love of God. Trust in the universe. Love will always prevail. Do not fear. Your love is all you need to get by. Have faith. Have love for yourself. You are a child of God, and can create your own reality. Do not fear. Have faith. Faith and love are all you will ever need. Be at peace.*

Angela already had faith in a God, but she hadn't known that God could speak to everyone directly. She thought God only spoke through the voices of prophets in spiritual texts.

Later she learned that God is in everything and everybody, so God could speak to her through every person on the Earth, and through all of his creation.

Be a Light unto the World

Angela had learned many lessons from the *Conversations With God* books, and she aspired to be just like Neale Donald Walsch. As she grew more comfortable with the idea of talking to God, she wanted to learn all there was to know about God, and to pass it on to all the world, so everyone could share in the knowledge. She found one particular extract especially inspiring:

> Be a light unto the world, and hurt it not…
>
> Make of your life a gift. Remember always, you are the gift!
>
> Be a gift to everyone who enters your life, and to everyone whose life you enter. Be careful not to enter another's life if you cannot be a gift.
>
> (You can always be a gift, because you always are a gift—yet sometimes you don't let yourself know that.)
>
> When someone enters your life unexpectedly, look for the gift that person has come to receive from you…
>
> I tell you this: every person who has ever come to you has come to receive a gift from you. In so doing, he gives a gift to you—the gift of your experiencing and fulfilling Who You Are.
>
> When you see this simple truth, when you understand it, you see the grandest truth of all:
>
> I HAVE SENT YOU
> NOTHING BUT ANGELS.[14]

The Little Soul

These books contained many lessons. One of the greatest lessons which Angela learned was to try not to judge others, because everyone is really one of God's angels. This concept was brought home to her by a delightful story, which God told in these books, of the Little Soul.

God told us about a Little Soul who wanted to experience itself as the light it knew itself to be. It could not do this in heaven where everyone else shone just as brightly, so God allowed the soul to separate from the rest of the light, in order to experience itself in contrast to the darkness. God advised the little soul to "be a light unto the darkness, and curse it not", and that "the experience you create is a statement of Who You Are—And Who You Want to Be"[15].

When God continued the story in a later conversation with Neale Donald Walsch, he advised the Little Soul that it was able to experience itself as any aspect of divinity it wanted to. The Little Soul decided it wanted to experience forgiveness, but all the other souls in heaven were just as perfect as it was, and it could not understand how it would find someone to forgive. Then the Friendly Soul stepped forward and offered to do something "bad", to allow the Little Soul to experience itself as forgiveness during its next physical life. The Friendly Soul offered to do something "bad" out of love for the Little Soul, and because the Little Soul had previously done the same for it. The Friendly Soul asked only one thing in return for this huge favour:

> "In the moment that I strike you and smite you," said the Friendly Soul, "in the moment that I do the worst to you that you could ever imagine—in that self-same moment ... remember Who I Really Am."
>
> "Oh, I won't forget!" promised the Little Soul. "I will see you in the perfection with which I hold you now, and I will remember Who You Are, always."[16]

Although Angela was not always successful at applying this lesson, it gave her something to work towards. It also allowed her to understand some of the other lessons that she had received.

She now understood one reason she should do unto others as she would have them do unto her, as she learned from all of the religions she studied. God had sent her nothing but angels, and those who strike and smite her were really being friendly souls allowing her to experience her divine self. She also knew now she no longer wished to experience being someone who needed to be forgiven.

Factory Farmed Animals

Angela felt guilty about eating meat after reading of the plight of factory-farmed animals, who suffer tremendously throughout their lives. The book, *Diet for a New America*[17], was recommended in *Conversations with God*. Although the book gave facts and figures relating to American factory farming, Angela knew the conditions for Australian factory farmed animals were no better. She asked Jesus about it.

Jesus: *Angela, you can know that your life is taking off now, but there are still many lessons for you to learn. One lesson is that you can love yourself, despite any perceived flaws that you have, just as you can love others who you perceive are flawed. You know that anyone is doing the best that they can in any given situation.*

Angela: How can I help to relieve the plight of our factory farmed animals?

Jesus: *You can care. You do care. Caring is the first step. Speaking out about your caring is the second step. Acting on your caring is the third step.*

Angela: How can I help others to understand the plight of our factory farmed animals without sounding judgemental?

Jesus: *Tell people of your feelings. They will understand that you are not judging them, but yourself. But understand that you have no more need to judge yourself than others. You can change the way you think, speak and act, and send your past mistakes to heaven as you have learned. Be a beacon of love and light to the world. Let the world know that your love extends to all the creatures of the earth, including factory-farmed animals. Be an example to others and you can achieve your aims of a world where all creatures, including humans, are treated with love and respect.*

Do not fear. Love will prevail. All will be well. Have faith.

Angela: I have the faith of a mustard seed, but sometimes I wonder if that's enough.

Jesus: *That is enough, Angela. Your faith will see you through. Your love will see you through. Go forth and tell the world about your love for all the creatures of the Earth. Your love will see you through. All the world will know that you are a beacon of love and light. Shine your light on the plight of the creatures whom you wish to help. Shine your love on the creatures, and you are already helping them. Be at peace.*

Angela: Please help me to send my love, my peace, my joy and my healing to all of the creatures who suffer at the hands of humankind.

Angela felt such love and joy and she sent all the love, joy, healing, and peace she could muster, out to all the creatures of the Earth—all the battery (caged) chickens, all the broiler (meat) chickens, the pigs, the cattle, the calves, all those anonymous, unknown creatures who are in pain because they make an extra dollar for their owners that way.

As she sent her love out into the world, Angela said a prayer for these creatures. She knew their owners did not understand the pain they caused, or if they did know, they felt trapped by circumstance. She prayed that, we, as a community, would find a way for all the creatures of the Earth and the owners of these factory farms to live happy, healthy lives and enjoy life as God intended.

Angela had forgotten the suffering of these animals, until she read *Diet for a New America*[17]. She realised that it is easy to put them out of our minds, when we talk of beef instead of cows, and pork instead of pigs.

She vowed never to forget their plight again.

> Jesus: *Angela, you can know that it is not necessary for you to be perfect. It is only necessary for you to care for the consequences of your actions. Your love will go a long way to remove the consequences for those that you send your love to. Your loving thoughts are powerful.*
>
> *When you send your love out into the world, it has a dramatic effect on all involved. Remember to love yourself first. Your love is a very powerful healer for both yourself and the world.*
>
> *When mistakes are made, send your mistakes to heaven as you have learned from the fairies. Remember that love is the key. Be not afraid. Your love is all you need to get by. You can send your love out into the world and all will be well. Remember to love yourself first.*

Send Your Mistakes to Heaven

Angela knew she had to buy Doreen Virtue's book, *Healing With The Fairies*[18], when she saw it on the same shelf as her latest set of tarot cards. As had often happened lately, this book all but jumped into her arms.

Later, Angela asked Allan if he could tell her something about fairies. Although, prior to her own experience of them, Angela had an open mind about angels and spirit guides, she had never previously considered the fact that fairies were real. She thought they were just the characters in 'fairy stories', based on someone's imagination.

> Allan: *Angela, fairies are your friends. They are sweet as honey and light as a feather. They appreciate your love as do all entities this side, but they will take your love and make it grow for you.*

Angela learned from the book that fairies are "God's guardian angels of nature, and they ensure the health and safety of animals, plants and Mother Earth"[18]. Although we can't always see them, fairies actually have a physical body, albeit a very light one, with many of the same needs as a human body.

Angela read that we can help the fairies by first believing in their existence. They apparently become more powerful, the more people believe in them. Also we can do our bit to care for the environment, to provide a better life for their charges, the plants and animals, and also to improve the conditions in which fairies live.

After remembering the plight of factory farmed animals, Angela resolved to change her habits in the future, but was excited to discover that the fairies in Doreen Virtue's book had advice on how to take care of her mistakes in the past:

As a human, the point is to be aware of your underlying intentions. As long as you intend to be loving, don't focus upon mistakes that you may make. When you make mistakes, give them to heaven.... Whenever you become aware that you have made a mistake, meaning an error in thinking based upon unloving or fearful thoughts, simply say, 'I admit that a mistake has been made, and I ask that all effects of these mistakes be undone in all directions of time for everyone concerned.'[18]

Angela learned that God lives in every one of us—every fairy, every human, animal, plant, grain of sand, and spirit. She learned that there is much more to life than she had realised, that miracles happen every day, but she hadn't before noticed them. She learned that the greatest miracle of all is the love that dwells within us all. For that is what God is.

Friends with God

Angela learned from another of Neale Donald Walsch's books, *Friendship With God*[19], that God could become her friend. She hadn't had many friends before she found God. She was pretty much a loner. She had a few people she cared about, but none that she could turn to with her troubles. She had Bill, of course, but she couldn't talk to him about any of her spiritual problems. Her best friends in school had either moved away or had been a bad influence on her, such that her parents forbade her from even speaking to them again. Her best adult friend had died prematurely. As a child and teenager, she was close to her sister, Beth, who was only fifteen months older than her, but they drifted apart. Beth also had some doubts about Angela's sanity, after her attempts at communicating with their deceased parents and friend. So Angela welcomed God's friendship with open arms and an open heart.

God explained to Angela that one reason she was reluctant to talk to him in the beginning was that she was afraid that he would let her down, as her other friends had. He promised that he would never let her down, that she could always rely on him. So she trusted him. She trusted him with her life and with her love.

In the book, *Friendship With God*[19], God advised that our basic nature as human beings is to be loving: to love everyone and everything, even though it is not normal for us to do so, because we have discouraged a lot of our natural behaviours, including enjoyment of sex, telling the truth, singing, dancing and celebration.

Angela read in the book: "Release the joy that is inside of another, and you release the joy that is inside of you" and that there are a "thousand times a thousand" ways to do this. God gave some examples ranging from "something as simple as a smile" to those which require more effort, like "the willingness to listen" and "the decision to forgive"[19].

Being joyful is the key, which is why, in the book, God put it first in the list of the "Five Attitudes of God": to be "totally joyful, loving, accepting, blessing and grateful". It is important to know the attitudes of God if you are to have a friendship with God, as God has given knowing God as the first of "Seven Steps to Friendship with God"[19]:

One: Know God
Two: Trust God
Three: Love God
Four: Embrace God
Five: Use God
Six: Help God
Seven: Thank God

The book advised that the first step in being fully loving is to fully love yourself. God warns, that "this you cannot do so long as you believe that you were born in sin, and are basically evil." God suggests that "this question—what is the basic nature of man?—is the most important question now before the human race." She suggests that the society that we create will be a result of whether we believe humans are basically "non-trustworthy and evil", or "trustworthy and good". If we believe that humans are non-trustworthy and evil, we will create a society that is "freedom *limiting*", rather than one which is "freedom *giving*"[19].

Angela knew that anyone who has travelled on an international aeroplane lately, and has been told "Sorry, you can't take that bottle of shampoo on board," will have no doubts about which direction our society is heading. Angela knew she didn't like her freedoms being eroded, but now she knew why—it is against human nature.

She thought: "Perhaps it is not too late to reverse the trend. We can start by trusting other people in all of our dealings with them. Expect the best of people, and it is quite possible that the best is what they will be."

Free Will is Paramount

After reading the book, Angela decided she would like to talk to her friend, God. She asked to communicate with highest vibrational guides only, as usual, and then said she actually wanted to talk to God.

> Angela: I wasn't sure if I need to ask for high vibrational guides only, if I only want to talk to God. Am I guaranteed to only get God if that is who I ask for?
>
> God: *Angela, there are no guarantees in this life, but God is always here to talk to you and to listen to you. Ask and you shall receive. I will never let you down.*
>
> Angela: Why are there no guarantees, then?
>
> God: *To guarantee that you would only get my communication may deny another being the right to communicate with you. As you learned from* Conversations With God, *I am not in the business of denying any being's rights. Free will is paramount.*
>
> Angela: Do I need to raise my vibration to hear your message?

God: *It is not necessary, but it helps you to focus your attention and to block your thoughts, so that my message is clearer.*

Angela: I didn't have anything in particular to ask. I just wanted to thank you for creating such a wonderful world. The beauty of it, the vastness of it, the wonder of it, was made apparent to me on our cruise. Thank you also for your love.

God: *You are welcome, Angela. My love is your love. You feel my love now as you focus on your love.*

Angela: I love you.

God: *I love you.*

Angela: Any other messages?

God: *Do not fear that problems may arise, that are insurmountable. You know that you are a creative being and you have the ability to move mountains. I have given you the ability to achieve all of your goals. Do not fear. All will be well.*

Angela: What happens when a situation arises that I don't desire? If there are no errors, then does this mean that I really did desire this situation—that is, that my higher self did, but just didn't let me know?

God: *Angela, you and your higher self are one being. If you are wanting something that is not in accordance with the desires of your higher self, then it is because you are not listening.*

You are right. There are no accidents. You have created all of your reality. Sometimes you know that it is in your best interests not to be totally aware of your higher self's desires, as it may defeat your aims. Have faith and trust in the universe to bring you all of your desires.

Meditate often. In the stillness, you will know the wishes of your higher self. Listen to your heart. Listen to your feelings. Remember that your feelings are the voice of your soul. Trust that I have created in you the perfect being, the perfect means of achieving your aim of remembering who you really are, and then assisting others to also remember.

Do not fear. Your ability to hear my message is real. I will let you know if there is an error. Have faith. Have love. All will be well. Be at peace.

Angela: God, I have been going through the seven steps to friendship with God. I think I am getting to know God, and I am learning to trust God. I definitely love God. I am not sure how to embrace God. I think I am using God. How can I help God? And I do thank God, perhaps not often enough. But thank you God, in advance now. Can you please tell me how to embrace God, and what help I can be?

God: *Angela, you can embrace God, by being the best that you can be. You can embrace God, by being your loving self. You can embrace God by acknowledging that you are a child of God, and therefore you are a creative being, just like God. You can embrace God by being you. As for helping God, you can help God in everything that you do. You can listen for my counsel. You can listen for the wee small voice within—your God connection.*

You can help God by loving yourself and all the world. You can help God by being you. You can help God by loving all you meet, all you see, all you hear of, and all you know of. You can help God by being love. Indeed, you are love, just as I am, just as everyone is, just as all of God's creation is.

You can help God by doing just what you are doing— listening, writing down my words, telling others of my words, telling others that they need not listen to your description of my words, but they can hear my words themselves. They can all have conversations with God, become friends with God, and be one with God. You are helping God. Thank you, Angela.

Angela: Thank you, God. Thank you for the enlightenment recently. I feel as though I have crossed a line, climbed a mountain, achieved a certain height.

God: *Yes, Angela, you have. But as you pointed out in your writing, there are more mountains to climb. Have no fear. I will be with you always, in every mountain climb, in all your endeavours. I love you and all the world. Go now and send your love, which is my love, out into the world. Think love in all that you do, and all will be well. Be at peace.*

Have Faith

A couple of days later, Angela had some financial decisions to make at work. She had to decide whether to pay some large bills that would leave the business with little to spare for emergencies. She felt that this would be the correct path to take, if she was trusting in God and the universe. Although Angela felt like it was the wrong thing to do, she chose the safe option and spoke to God that evening.

Angela: Hello, God. I wanted to ask you about the saying I heard recently—"Trust in God, but tie up your camel." Surely if we can really put our faith in God, we wouldn't need to tie our camels, would we? I thought of this today, so I didn't go further out on that limb we spoke of the other day.

God: *No, Angela, and you have deduced the reason why tying your camel is necessary. Tying your camel is only necessary if you don't believe that I and the universe can deliver. You were right in your thinking that I cannot control your camel, any more than I can control your dog. All creatures have free will to stay or go. But if you trust in the universe to bring you all of your desires, both yours and your camel's desires can be met. Faith is the key. 'Trust in*

God, but tie up your camel' is definitely the correct way to think if you lack faith.

Angela: You said yourself there are no guarantees in this life. How can we put our trust in a God, in a universe, that can't provide guarantees?

God: *You are right, Angela. There are no guarantees in life, but your faith can lead you to your desires. The universe has at its disposal such means that you may not be aware of. There is always a way for your desires to come to you, and the universe is bound to find a way. But free will is paramount. Have faith that the universe can find a way to satisfy everyone's desires, whilst maintaining free will for everyone. Believe and it is so.*

Angela: So, what you're saying, in effect, is if I don't tie the camel and believe the camel is right back there when I need it, the universe must oblige, even if the camel chooses to take a wander.

God: *Yes, Angela. You cannot see how you and your camel can both get what you want. This is where faith comes in. Have faith and believe in the universe, and all will be well.*

Angela: So what you are saying, God, is that, had I gone further out on that limb today, the universe would have to find a way to support me, as long as I believe it can.

God: *That is right, Angela. Trust in God, trust in the universe, and your camel will take care of itself. Obviously it is easier for the universe to oblige if you keep your desires general—relating to the outcome, rather than the means to that outcome. For example, if you said you didn't want to tie your camel, and you need to have a ride home, but didn't care how you got there, as long as your camel appeared at some stage, this would give the universe greater scope to oblige you and your camel. The more specific your desires, the more work the universe must do to achieve those desires, but anything is possible, given enough faith.*

Angela: Anything is possible, but not guaranteed?

God: *That is correct. Angela you came into this world with certain goals. You may not be aware of your soul's goals in this life, so guarantees are not always possible, but with faith all things are possible.*

Angela: It sounds a bit like a cop-out, God. If I desire something, and it doesn't happen, you can say my soul didn't want it so.

God: *Angela, you know that you and your soul are one being, as we have discussed before. Your soul can let you know its desires if you will but listen. During meditation, your soul is much easier to hear.*

Angela: God, I am having trouble here.

God: *I know, Angela. You can't put faith in a God that won't give you guarantees. But have I not told you also, that I will never let you down?*

Angela: Yes, but aren't these two statements contradictory?

God: *Only without faith. Faith is the key. For those who have faith, anything is possible. All of the miracles that you were reading about this morning would be impossible without faith. As you read, miracles happen all the time. Jesus performed many miracles with ease, because of his faith. Have I not told you that you are a creative being, and you can create your own reality. Ask and you shall receive. Seek and you shall find. Knock and the door shall be opened unto you. Believe and it is so. Have faith and all will be well.*

Angela: So you think I should go further out on that limb and have faith.

God: *You know that I am not going to tell you what you should do, Angela. Free will is paramount. I can tell you that I will never let you down. My love for you is eternal. My love for you is real. Have faith and all will be well. Have love. Have faith. Be at peace.*

Miracles

One Sunday morning Angela rose unusually early, and noticed that the rain, which had been forecast to fall overnight, had not eventuated. Everything was starting to look very dry, so she was a little disappointed. She said to herself, "I wish we could have some rain."

A couple of minutes later she heard heavy raindrops hit the roof. She thought it was strange, because it seemed like a sunny day. She went outside and looked up into the sky. Apart from a couple of small wispy clouds off to one side, it was a clear blue sky. It only rained for a few minutes, but it was enough to convince her another miracle had occurred.

She knew a weather expert could probably give her a logical explanation for rain falling from a clear blue sky, but for her it was further evidence that miracles happen every day, and we can all be the creators of them. We just have to believe it's possible. Another day, Bill was complaining loudly at his computer. He relied on his computer for everything and this time it stopped working and he couldn't get it going again. Angela spoke to God during her meditation.

Angela: God, do you think it would be ok to get Bill's computer working again?

God: *Angela, you know I am God and all things are possible for God, as you found out the other day when you asked me to get the mouse working again. I did, did I not?*

Angela: You certainly did. Thank you.

God: *Believe it and it is so. You are a creative being. You are a child of God, and you have the same creative powers that God has. Have I not told you that, with the faith of a mustard seed, you can move mountains.*

Angela: Yes, God. I have faith of a mustard seed, but sometimes my doubt seems greater than the size of a mustard seed.

God: *Indeed, your doubt can sometimes cancel out your faith. But have faith and all will be well.*

After Angela finished her meditation session, she went out to see if Bill's computer was fixed, and sure enough, it was working again. She told him that God and she had fixed it for him. Unfortunately, he didn't believe her, which could be why it failed again a couple of days later. However, the mouse, which God had fixed at Angela's request a few days earlier, was still going strong.

Angela: God, I wanted to know about whether it is a problem to ask you for help with trivial things all the time. I know miracles happen every day, but is it wrong to ask for a lot of little miracles—like when I asked you to fix my mouse? Most people normally only ask for help with the big stuff—life and death matters. Are we being pesky pests asking for help with the little things?

God: *Lots of little things can a big thing make. The many small loaves and fishes, with which Jesus fed the multitude, were a lot of little things, but the story of his miracles lives on to this day, and that is a big thing. You know that you, too, can create miracles if you believe it so. Asking for my help is not a problem. Nothing is too difficult for God. Nothing is too small. Nothing is too large. I am happy to help with any difficulties you may face, but remember, if you keep a positive outlook you can reduce the number of difficulties you encounter. If you keep a positive outlook, you may not need any help.*

But remember what I was saying about getting too bogged down in the detail. If you keep your desires more general, and keep focused on the outcome you desire, that outcome will come to you more quickly, than if you focus on the minute means to achieve that outcome. But help is always available.

Angela had read all about Jesus' miracles feeding the multitudes and raising Lazarus from the dead. She even thought of her mouse as a sort of mini-Lazarus. But still her faith was not always strong.

She asked for help from God to increase her faith. She was grateful for the help she received in many areas.

Planning for The Future

Angela: God, it is difficult to live in the moment and address the future of our business and the future of our staff's lives.

God: *If you consider the future of the business, and your staff's lives, from the position of your present moment, you will find there is nothing to fear. You can plan for the future, and still keep yourself firmly in the present.*

Angela: But the problem I have is I don't know how to plan for the future. There are too many unknowns, and

I know I should be thinking life is easy, and it will be. But at the moment, when I look to plan the future, it seems much too hard.

God: *Angela, if you don't have enough information to plan for the future, then you can't plan. You can only worry. Stay in your present moment until you have all the information you need, and then plan.*

Angela: Ok God. I'll try. Also, I wanted to let you know that the thinking love thing did work to a certain extent, but didn't seem to completely remove any difficulties.

God: *Yes, Angela, it did, but only in your present moment. Love in your present moment will definitely remove any difficulties from that moment. This is why it is necessary to remain present, only looking forward from your secure position in the present, and then only when you have all the information you need to plan, or to visualise the future you want, but visualise it as if it was in the present, and then always returning to the present. The present moment holds all the love, all the joy, you could ever want.*

Live in the moment, and all will be well. Have faith in the universe to bring you all of your desires, and think love before all that you do, and if in doubt of what to do, ask, 'What would love do now?' and follow the answer. It is easy.

Talking to God regularly was a gradual process. She preferred to talk to him with a pen and notebook in hand, as she had with Jesus and her other spiritual friends before him. She did talk to God, as she would a friend, as she walked up the street, or attended to her housework, but she could never be sure that the words she heard were God's and not hers, so she kept all serious matters for written conversations.

They talked about many things—about her day, about her problems, about life. God told her what her life would be like in the future, about how she would write a book and have it published, and become God's confident, faithful, invincible beacon, and she believed him.

Although not all of Angela's lessons were painful, there were many which challenged her, especially in the relating of them. She hoped sharing these lessons would, one day, release joy in others, and thus in herself.

If someone had told Angela a few years ago, that she would be embarrassed to talk about love, she probably wouldn't have believed them. But back then, she hadn't really thought much about love, and had certainly never experienced the love she was soon to discover.

Lessons of Love

Love Yourself First

Late one Saturday afternoon, Angela intended to do an early meditation but felt very sexy, and knew that her increased vibration would make her even more so. She decided to have a sensual bath by candlelight. Of course, she did in the bath what people, from babies to geriatrics, have done in the bath since the bath was invented.

Bill was busy in the office doing something on the computer. She felt silly about it, but Angela was a bit embarrassed about what she was doing, and didn't want to be caught in the act. The closed door of the bathroom meant Bill was unaware of her activities; not so, her spiritual helpers.

Later that evening, Angela spoke to Jesus, after he had helped her with her healing.

> Angela: Jesus, I wanted to thank you for your healing help. Are there any messages for me?
>
> Jesus: *You're welcome, Angela. Yes, I do have a message. Do not fear loving yourself, for you are a child of God, and*

God loves you as his child. Therefore you are definitely worthy of love from everyone, including yourself. You felt the pleasure that loving yourself can bring, both emotionally and physically. Love is never anything to be embarrassed about, or to fear.

Angela: I know you are right, Jesus. But we have been conditioned to believe we shouldn't love ourselves, only others.

Jesus: *Yes, Angela, but you do not need to carry on the tradition. God's first rule is 'Love yourself first' and from that position of loving yourself, you can much more easily love others. In fact, it is very difficult to truly love others, if you do not love yourself first. Never fear. Love is here. You can always love yourself, in any situation. Love is the key to any situation.*

Angela asked to speak to God as well.

Angela: God, I just wanted to tell you I love you.

God: *And I love you, Angela. Jesus is right. There is nothing to fear in loving yourself. You know we love you. It is important to love yourself before loving others. This is the case both physically, and emotionally. Love for yourself can be shared with others. What you give, you receive, so love for yourself is a closed loop. Once you love yourself, you really want to share that love. Once you feel love, you can't help but want to share it. But you have to feel it first, which is why it is important to love yourself first.*

The next morning, following her brief meditation, God asked to speak to her.

God: *Angela, I wanted to tell you I love you, but I also wanted to tell you to love yourself. You are being a bit hard on yourself, because you think you did not write our messages exactly word perfectly last night. You can know that you got the gist of it right.*

We were saying that it is ok to love yourself. In fact it is necessary to love yourself, if you truly want to love another. This applies to physical and emotional love. There is never a reason to fear love or to fear talking about love, whether it is spiritual, emotional, or physical love. All love is to be cherished.

Your love is a great gift from God, and it is a wonderful gift to share. But to share your love, you first have to feel love, so you have to love yourself first. That is the way it works. Once you can feel love in yourself, you can share it with others.

Never fear love, for love is all there is. Love will get you through any difficulties. Love is the light of the world. Go now and love yourself, and whomever you wish to share your love with, but remember to love yourself first.

Also remember, Angela, you are doing a wonderful job of transcribing our messages. You should not fear if you make a slight mistake. We will let you know if you make a mistake, otherwise you have got the gist of what we are saying. Have confidence in your abilities. You are doing well. Go now and be a beacon of love and light to the world, but remember to love yourself first.

Talk about Sex

Although Angela was not keen on discussing it, God had more to say on the subject of physical love when they spoke again.

God: *Angela, I wanted to talk to you about sex. You know you have some inhibitions in relation to talking about sex and loving yourself physically. You can also know, Angela, you are not the only one. Many in your society, and throughout the world, have difficulty talking about sex and other physical forms of love. Although sex is often on people's minds, they feel inhibited when talking about it. What I would like to see, Angela, is people talking about sex more often. Talk about it with Bill, but also talk about it within your wider society.*

Angela: I'll try, God, but why do you ask this?

God: *These inhibitions, Angela, can lead to many problems, both in relationships, and in society. The more you talk about sex, the more you can talk about it. This can lead to breaking down these inhibitions, and thus breaking down the problems they cause.*

The next day, Angela was troubled. She spoke to Jesus that evening.

> Jesus: *Angela, I wanted to talk to you about your day. You were feeling a bit down today. Do you know why?*
>
> Angela: Not really, Jesus. Do you?
>
> Jesus: *Yes, Angela. You have lost some of your faith. You are perhaps wondering if you made up your conversation with God last night, if you might, in fact, be crazy after all.*
>
> Angela: Yes, I guess that could cause me to be a bit down, and yes, that thought has flitted through my mind from time to time.
>
> Jesus: *Angela, you know you aren't crazy. God's message to you is real. You know God is real. You know I am real. You know the things God told you last night were not in your mind prior to your conversation. You know that the ideas expressed were not your thoughts.*
>
> Angela: Ah, but who knows what my subconscious thinks?
>
> Jesus: *I do, Angela, and it doesn't think that.*

Angela: Ok, Jesus, I believe you.

Jesus: *Angela, you know our love for you is real. You have felt it.*

Angela: Yes, Jesus, I have. I'm sorry.

Jesus: *No need to be sorry, Angela. You are only human. It is normal for you to have doubts about the origins of these messages. Not long ago, you would have thought anyone very weird if they said they were having conversations with Jesus and God.*

Angela: And I still do. But now I include myself in that.

Jesus: *Yes, Angela, but you know we are real. You know deep down we are all one. You know this is the reason you can hear our messages. Because we are all one. You know that.*

Angela: I do, Jesus. I love you.

Jesus: *I know you do, Angela…when you believe in me.*

Angela: Yes, right.

Jesus: *You feel better now, don't you?*

Angela: Yes, Jesus, because you have reminded me, once again, who I am.

Jesus: *Yes, Angela, that is what we are all here for—to remind each other of who we are—children of God, all part of God's love.*

Angela: Thanks, Jesus.

Angela knew Jesus was right. She had been doubting the origins of these messages. She had trouble talking about sex and loving herself physically, so she found it difficult to imagine God and Jesus would want to talk about it.

So perhaps here was evidence this couldn't possibly be coming from her mind, because to her mind, these were things one didn't speak of.

Love is All There is

After another amazing healing the following evening, Angela spoke to Jesus again.

Angela: Wow again, Jesus.

Jesus: *Wow is right, Angela.*

Angela: Thanks Jesus.

Jesus: *You're welcome, Angela. I wanted to tell you that it is a totally natural thing, Angela, for you to think sexual thoughts when your vibration is raised, and to want to pleasure yourself physically. The increased vibration you feel causes all of your body to vibrate, as you deduced previously. It does work just like a vibrator, but it also causes you to want to love yourself, and all of creation. You can love yourself physically much more easily than the rest of creation, but if the rest of creation was with you, you would want to love us all physically as well. It is a perfectly natural thing to want to share the love you receive, physically, emotionally, and spiritually.*

You can know you are doing a wonderful job of transcribing our messages. As God has told you, if there is an error, we will let you know. Otherwise, you can know you have got the gist of it.

Your love is a great gift from God. As you have discovered this afternoon, if you don't fear love, but openly display your love for yourself, it can lead to loving of others. Remember, you need to love yourself first, before sharing your love with others. But as you discovered, it is something easily shared, if you love yourself first. Your love is all you need in any circumstances.

Your love can bridge the gap between lovers, who are too busy to get together; it can bridge the gap between two people, two countries, two cultures. It can bridge any gap, solve any problem, forge any stream. Love can hold back the tides, and can be a beacon to all the world. Love is a truly remarkable gift from God, which all of his creation has in common. It is the link between two lovers, two enemies, two nations, two worlds. Love is all that matters, and love is the key to all problems.

Be a beacon of love and light to all the world. Shed your light on the love that surrounds you, on the love that is you and all of God's creation. Be a beacon of love and light, and all the world benefits.

There is nothing to fear in love, ever. Love yourself, or the one you are with, or the whole world. Love is a wonderful thing to receive, and to share.

Angela, you can go now and share your love with the rest of the world, in the form of your peace, love, healing, and joy, that you send out to all the world. Love yourself first, and then the world. Love the one you're with, and whomever you choose. Be at peace.

After sending her love out into the world, Angela spoke to God.

God: *Love truly is a wonderful thing, isn't it?*

Angela: Yes, God. Love is lovely.

God: *It is, Angela. Love is pure bliss. Love is pure joy. Love is all there is. Love is the up and the down, the in and the out, the Earth, the stars, the universe. Love is all there is. You are pure love, as is all of my creation. There is nothing to fear in any situation, for in any situation you are surrounded by love.*

Love will see you through any difficulties. Love will give you peace, joy, and healing, and love will help you climb the highest mountain or write the most difficult book. Love is pure magic. Love is divine. You are divine, as is all of my creation.

Be a beacon of love and light to all the world. Have no fear. Love is here, always. Love is all there is. Be a beacon of love and light, and shine your light on the love that surrounds you. Be at peace.

Although Angela didn't enjoy speaking about physical love, she was happy to experience it. When her vibration was raised, she enjoyed loving herself, and was grateful when it led to her being able to share her love with Bill, as she had yesterday. Jesus was right; previously, they were too busy to get together, but she hoped yesterday was an indication of what things might be like in the future.

Love = Vibration = Healing = Sex

The next day, Angela asked Allan to explain the link between love and vibration.

> Allan: *Your vibration is a measure of your love. If you are filled with vibration, you are filled with love.*
>
> Angela: Can I not have a low vibration and be filled with love?
>
> Allan: *You can, but you can experience it more easily in a high vibrational state. When you are in a high vibrational state, you are closer spiritually to the love you experience. You are also closer mentally and physically.*

Angela: So, if we all raise our vibrations, we will love each other more?

Allan: *Yes, Angela. As you found, you want to share your love with everyone.*

Angela: I thought we needed to be in a lower vibration to exist on the Earth.

Allan: *But you can raise your vibration to a high level and still exist happily in body, mind and spirit. The higher the vibration, the closer vibrationally to the spiritual realm, but you can exist in the physical realm with a raised vibration.*

Angela: It can be a bit distracting.

Allan: *Yes, Angela. Which is why you learn to control your vibration. You can raise it when you want to and lower it when you want to.*

Angela: It seems harsh to have to choose between a full experience of love and living comfortably in the world.

Allan: *You can have both, just not at the same time. A full experience of love is distracting because it allows you to realise that love is all there is, and all you want to have and do. This is why you can't have a full experience of love continuously, but you can have a nearly full experience of love and still exist comfortably in the world. A nearly full experience of love, with the occasional lift into the full experience.*

Angela: I feel like there are more questions, but can't think what they are.

Allan: *You want to know the link between love and healing, and love and sex, and love and vibration. They are all one. Just as we are all one, all of the expressions of love are one and the same. Love is vibration, is sex, is healing. Give any of these and you give the other. Sex is physical love. Vibration is energetic love. Healing is a form of energetic and physical love combined. As you have learned, you can love yourself by giving vibration to your body. You can love others by sending your loving vibration, your loving energy out in the form of healing, or you can give your loving energy physically in the form of sex between a couple.*

Angela: So you are saying there is no such thing as sex without love?

Allan: *Sex without love is a physical impossibility. Sometimes you are only loving yourself with sex; sometimes you are loving both yourself and the other. Always there is love.*

Angela: What about between prostitute and client, or in the case of rape?

Allan: *In the case of rape, the instigator is forcing the other person to give love they don't want to give. It is still a loving act, but neither party is experiencing love, because you can't experience love which is forcibly taken or which is forcibly given. Love is there, but neither party experiences it. A similar situation applies with a prostitute to a lesser degree, as love is given, but not freely.*

Feeling the Love of God

As well as talking about love, God gave Angela many demonstrations of her love.

> Angela: Hello, God. What did you want to talk about?
>
> God: *Let's not talk, Angela. Let's make love. Let's both of us feel each other's love.*
>
> Angela: Ok, God. Did you want to put this in the book?
>
> God: *Yes please, Angela.*
>
> …

Angela writhed with joy as the loving vibration and pleasurable feelings filled her body from head to toe.

> Angela: Thank you, God. I love you.
>
> God: *And I love you, Angela. Did you want to tell me what you felt?*
>
> Angela: You know what I felt.
>
> God: *Yes, but your readers don't.*

Angela: Ok, God. I felt lots of love, lots of vibration, and I felt a need to love myself physically.

God: *Yes, Angela, as Jesus was telling you before, you would like to share the love that you feel with someone, but you are the only person present, so you are the only one you can love physically.*

Angela: Ok, God, and what did you feel?

God: *I felt all you felt, Angela, but much, much, more. I felt my love vibrate in you, and I felt your need to share your love, and then I felt your love come back to me, and my love go back to you. It is a wonderful closed loop of vibrational love, that could go on and on forever if we let it.*

Angela: God, this does feel glorious, but I don't understand the reason you want to tell the world about it.

God: *I want to tell the world, Angela, because I would love it if all the world could feel what we feel, could share what we share. I would love to love the rest of humanity the way I have just loved you. I would love it if the rest of humanity could love me the way you do. Not for my sake, but for theirs. You know my love makes you feel wonderful.*

Angela: It does, God. It is only the talking about it that makes me feel a bit awkward.

God: *Which is all the more reason to talk about it. As I said before about sex, and the same applies to all forms of love—the more you talk about it, the more you can talk about it.*

Angela: I would love it if the rest of humanity loved you the way I do, too, God, or more even.

God: *What a joyous day that would be, Angela, and you are helping to bring that day closer to being.*

It was not surprising that Angela came to love God with all her heart, because God filled her heart with love.

Ecstasy

Angela: Hello, God. Did you want to talk to me?

God: *Yes, Angela. I wanted to tell you how much I love you, and all of my creation. Do not fear. All will be well. You have felt the power of love, have you not?*

Angela: I have, God. I have felt your love course through me, when you tell me you love me. I have felt my love being returned tenfold, as I send it out into the world. I have felt the power of love course through my hands during a healing. I feel it now as I vibrate, and sink into a well of honey. It is hard to describe, but it is close to ecstasy.

God: *Yes, Angela, it is close to ecstasy. Ecstasy is pure love expressed, pure love felt.*

Angela's mind went blank as the ecstasy overwhelmed her entire being.

...

Angela: Sorry, God, I lost you for a minute.

God: *Yes, Angela. You were busy feeling, and not busy listening. Even you, as a woman who can do multiple tasks, have a hard time doing other things when you sink into that honey of pure love, which is ecstasy. Your love will see you through any difficulties, but it will also give you great pleasure. Never fear. Your love is all you ever need to get by.*

Angela, as well as letting you feel my love again, which I know you enjoyed, I wanted to tell you, as well, how much I love you.

(This came in the form of the song.)
My love is warmer than the warmest sunshine, softer than a sigh.
My love is deeper than the deepest ocean, wider than the sky.
My love is brighter than the brightest star that shines every night above, and there is nothing in this world that can ever change my love.[20]

Angela: Oh, God. Just when I think I have felt the extent of your love, I am surprised yet again. I am sinking into that…vat of honey, again…

I feel like my heart is about to explode. I feel so very much alive. I feel ecstatic. I feel great joy…

Was there anything else, God?

God: *No, Angela, love is all there is.*

…

Angela: So, I'll go then, God.

God: *Yes, Angela. Go now, and take my love with you. Remember, I can open the floodgates any time you ask.*

Angela: Thanks, God. I love you.

…

Angela: I can't move, God. I am overwhelmed yet again.

God: *There's no hurry, Angela. You can stay in the honey a bit longer, if you wish.*

Angela felt the loving vibration coursing through her body, and she desperately wanted to share it with someone. She wanted to share it with her husband, Bill, but she believed he had become so disconnected from the love within himself, he was unable to accept the love she so wanted to give him. So she loved herself physically, and she prayed, again, for a change in Bill.

Love is Invincible

The following evening, after another amazing healing session with Jesus, and then loving the world, Angela spoke to God.

> Angela: It is easy to believe that anyone is invincible when they feel such a dramatic amount of love.
>
> God: *Yes, Angela. You are invincible just with your own love, but when you share your love with so many, you are right, there's no beating you. Angela, love will always prevail in any circumstances, so yes, love is always invincible. That is why thinking love will get you past any difficulties. Love overrides difficulties; love overrides everything. There is nothing love can't conquer—no problem, no difficulty, no mountain.*
>
> *Go now, and love yourself, or your lover, or the world. Love the one you're with, or yourself. You are a beacon of love and light in all that you do. That includes physical love, as well. You can shed your love and light on the joy and pleasure of physical love, on the joy and pleasure of emotional love, on the joy and pleasure of spiritual love. Love is all you will ever need. Be at peace.*

Waking up with Love

God allowed Angela to feel his love many times, and she began to realise that when she felt such love, she had no option but to return it. She began to love God with all her heart, with all her mind, with all her soul, and even with all her body.

> God: *Hello, Angela. How was your day?*
>
> Angela: I felt glorious for most of the day, God, thanks to you.
>
> God: *Nothing to do with me, Angela. That was your love you felt all day.*
>
> Angela: Why did I feel it more today, God? I'm not sure really.
>
> God: *Well, Angela, you were right in what you were just thinking. You went to sleep loving yourself, and feeling my love for you and your love for yourself, which spilled over onto all of creation. This love stayed with you during your sleep, and you woke up with love in your heart, and love on your mind. This allowed you to feel your love at the beginning of the day, which allowed you to feel your love more throughout your day. As you loved others, your love was returned to you, and you were able to keep the loving feeling most of the day.*

Your day was an example of that snowball effect I spoke of. If you can go to sleep with love, you are more likely to wake up with love, and more likely to spread your love throughout the day. Others then take your love and spread it to others again, so your love grows as it spreads. Your snowball grows and grows, affecting more and more people—all because you went to sleep with love.

Angela: Well, if that's the case, I should aim to go to sleep with love every night.

God: *Yes, Angela, that would be a good aim.*

Following their frank discussions about love, Angela felt no secrets between her and God now, and as she wrote about love in her book, she felt like she would have few secrets from her readers as well. She knew all her readers are part of God, and God is part of them, and we are all one, so that seemed reasonable. But she found this was one of the highest mountains to date—one of the most difficult for her to climb. It may not be quite to the height of Everest, but perhaps K2, and she knew it had to be done. She knew if she could make this difficult climb, then others would find it easier when they made the same ascent.

Angela wasn't sure what they teach in sex education classes nowadays, but in her day, nothing was taught about loving yourself first before sharing your love. In fact, they didn't have sex education classes in her day. Maybe that's the reason it was so difficult for her to talk about it now.

Prior to her awakening, Angela felt awkward even hugging a friend or relative. Yet, now she was determined to be God's confident, faithful, invincible beacon. She envisaged the new Angela being a loving person who could, not only give love in all of its forms, but could talk about it as well.

More Demonstrations of Love

Angela: Hello, God. I just got the urge to come and talk to you.

God: *I know, Angela. That was my doing.*

Angela: What did you want to tell me?

God: *I didn't, Angela. I wanted you to feel my love again, so you can write some more in your book about how glorious love is.*

…

Angela: I'm not doing much writing, God.

God: *I noticed, Angela.*

…

Angela: I am doing a lot of heavy sighing and moaning, though.

…

Angela: I feel my vibration increasing, and I am reminded of the Divinyls' song "I Touch Myself" but it is when I feel your love inside me, throughout me. God, you complete me, your love does, at least. Your love makes me feel as though I have everything I need within me. Your love makes me feel deliciously sensual, like I could hear, see, feel, taste, and smell everything much more wonderfully, much more intensely. Your love makes me feel as though I need nothing else in my life, and yet it makes me feel as though I would love to share it with everyone and everything. Your love feels glorious, God.

Was that the sort of thing you had in mind, God?

God: *Yes, Angela, but there is more.*

Angela: Well, God, your love is so overwhelming, it completely takes my mind off everything else, so all my problems disappear. Actually, I can't think of any problems now. And I feel such love for you, and all of your creation, God. I love everyone, including myself. And I feel like I could move mountains.

Was that what you had in mind?

God: *Yes, Angela. That is exactly what I had in mind. With my love and your love combined, you can indeed move mountains. You can make mountains disappear entirely. With our combined love, those molehills you had turned into mountains will turn back into molehills again.*

Angela: But I wonder, God, if I have not become more obsessed with the physical effects of your love than others may be. Should I leave that out of the book?

God: *No, Angela. You are a little embarrassed about telling the world about your loving yourself physically, but have we not told you that it is quite a natural reaction to your raised vibration? As you found last night, it is up to you whether or not you follow through with that reaction or not, but do not be afraid of the truth of your feelings.*

My love makes you want to share your love physically, when it causes you such a raised vibration. As Jesus explained, if you are the only one around, then it is natural that you will want to express love physically to yourself. You will know when it is appropriate to celebrate your physical love for yourself, and for others. As you discovered previously, even sharing a hug with another fulfills the desire to love another physically. But it is entirely natural, and as you have learned previously, the more you can talk about your physical love for yourself, the more you can talk about your physical love for yourself. The more you can talk about all forms of love, the easier it will be to practise all forms of love.

Have no fear, Angela. By the time this part of your book is read by others, you will have built up more self-confidence, and much more ability to talk about these things without them embarrassing you too much. Have faith and all will be well.

Angela: Ok, God. Thanks for the love.

God: *You're welcome, Angela. I love you all the time, but I only allow you to feel a small amount of my love normally, because, as you have said, it can be overwhelming. But know that any time you wish to experience more of my love, you can just ask, and I will open the floodgates for you.*

Angela knew God wanted her to tell her readers about these demonstrations of his love, so she was happy to receive a reminder. She knew God wanted her to give her readers more detail of her feelings, but as God had told her, words cannot describe the overwhelming feeling, the immensity of love God can feel, and therefore cause us to feel.

How could she describe her feelings of intense vibration, of such joy, of ecstasy, and love, that the world around disappeared? No, she dissolved into that feeling, and only love was left. She knew her description couldn't do God justice, and this was one of those things readers have to experience for themselves. They can ask and they shall receive.

God: *Hello, Angela. I wanted to say hello by allowing you to feel my love, which is taking you pretty close to that bliss you were going to ask about.*

Angela: Yes, God, but you know when I am so close to that bliss, I have trouble thinking of any questions, or anything else, for that matter.

God: *I know, Angela. It is wonderful, isn't it?*

Angela: It is, God. God, you said some can move into and out of bliss at will. Is that in the physical and the spirit planes?

God: *Yes, Angela. That is right.*

Angela: God, I have learned that raising my vibration takes me closer to the source, but I thought those of the spirit realm had higher vibrations normally. So, would they not be closer to bliss normally?

God: *Yes, Angela. They are closer, but not necessarily more able to move in and out of it at will. This takes a certain amount of training for those on that side as well. You have been fortunate to have experienced this merging on a few occasions now, if only briefly, but some beings have learned to come and stay for a while, and then go back to what they were doing or being.*

Angela: How can I get to that, God?

God: *Ask and you shall receive, Angela. You know that you have had help each time you have achieved this state, and you would probably need help to achieve this state again in the short term, but as in all things, practice makes perfect. Once you have experienced this a few times, and have felt how it feels to get to this state, you will be more capable of bringing yourself to that state.*

Angela: So this state of bliss is available to anyone who asks?

God: *Yes, Angela. They may need some preparatory steps beforehand, but perseverance and love will get them to their goals, and like you, once they have achieved that goal, they would be likely to want to experience that again.*

She was happy to learn about love, and grateful to receive demonstrations, but as these demonstrations continued, Angela began to have questions about the meaning of life, and what it was like in the spirit realm.

She had felt the urge to buy another Neale Donald Walsch book a few weeks before, and as she sat contemplating life and death, she noticed the book on her coffee table.

She picked it up and began to read.

Home With God[21]

Life and the Afterlife

The book, *Home with God*[21], contained a lot of answers for Angela, but, as often happens, it brought up some questions as well. The book guided Angela gently through the process of physical life and death. It explained life and the afterlife through a metaphor of a sphere, which is, on one side, an apple, representing physical life, with its core being the point of birth and death. Because the spiritual realm on the other side of the core is so different from the physical side, the metaphor described that side as being more like an orange. The sphere thus received the name of Applorange.

God asks you to…

> …imagine that you are an infinitesimal microbe, small but very much alive, moving through a tunnel in this apple.
>
> In this metaphor the walls of the 'tunnel' are the Corridors of Time. Along the corridor are markings that make each millimeter of wall different from any other…Now notice as you move through this tunnel that time is not passing. YOU are passing through TIME.[21]

This describes your physical life. Upon reaching the end of your physical life, you pass through the core, which is where you find The Singularity.

> At the Core of Your Being, All That Is and All That You Are appears in Singular Form. It is here that Knowing and Experiencing merge...
>
> You enter the Core of Your Being following what you call "death" in order to re-establish your identity. You move through the spiritual realm and through that process come to Know Again who and what you are, in fullness. You return to the Core of Your Being prior to what you call "birth" to re-create your identity anew, in the next grandest version of the greatest vision ever you held about Who You Are. That is, you elevate your experience and expression of Self, moving it to the next level. This is called evolution. You live your life in the physical world, that you might Know your Self in your own Experience.[21]

Angela could now answer one of the questions she had asked herself many years ago: what is life all about? She now knew that the purpose of her physical life was to experience herself as the person she had decided to be when she had been in the afterlife. She also knew that before her birth into a physical life and following her leaving it, she merged with All That Is—God.

Emotional Pain

Angela: God, I have found *Home with God*[21], both enlightening and confronting. I haven't finished it yet, but at times I felt such clarity and joy, and at others, confusion and anger. I think my confusion comes from trying to comprehend the meaning of life. When I can just be, I can be joyful with you. But then I try to understand the point of it all, and it becomes confusing. I can understand that one would want to have eternal life if it was joyful, but so many lives are filled with pain. It all seems too hard. It seems as though one would want to go to heaven to become joyful, then it seems one has to come back to the pain of life again.

God: *Angela, life need never be painful. I know a lot of people experience it that way. But you know they are creating their own reality. Many souls have decided that certain elements of life need to be painful in order to experience that part of their divine selves, but they and you need never experience pain if you do not wish to.*

Angela: But if my higher self decides that pain is required for me to experience something, then pain is what I will experience. I cannot change that, can I?

God: *Yes, Angela. You are a creative being and you never need to experience pain if you don't wish to. All of life can be experienced as joyful. Make the decision now to request constant joy and that is what you will receive.*

Angela: I think I have asked for that previously.

God: *Yes, Angela, but you didn't believe you could achieve it. Ask for it, and believe it is possible, and it can be yours.*

Angela: Ok. Constant joy can be mine from this point forward in my life. Joy, happiness, other feelings, but never emotional pain.

God: *Remember to be careful what you ask for, because you may just get what you want. Life is a rich tapestry of feelings, of emotions. Wishing for only one emotion is like changing the tapestry to be only one colour.*

In that instant, Angela suddenly had an awareness of what that joyful but dull tapestry would be like, and realised it wasn't what she wanted.

Angela: Yes, God, I see. You are right. How about asking that emotional pain be kept to a very minimum?

God: *That could work.*

100 Virgins

The next day, Angela met up with her sister, Beth, and an old friend of theirs over coffee. They had a long conversation which at one stage drifted towards death. Angela related what she had learned from *Home with God*[21] about the three stages of death.

In the first stage, you realise you are not your body— but you are still very much alive. In the second stage, in which you can remain for as long as you wish, you experience whatever you expect to experience—heaven, or hell, loved ones waiting for you, or nothing at all. (God did point out that there is no suffering in the afterlife, so even if you are expecting hell, your experience of it will not cause you suffering.) In the third stage of death, you merge with the Core of Your Being, with the Singularity, with the All.

When Angela mentioned about the stage where you experience what you expect to experience, her friend asked if suicide bombers experienced their 100 virgins.

"I guess," was Angela's reply.

Angela asked God about it that evening.

> Angela: God, can you please answer the question posed to me today? I was asked if Muslim terrorists—who believe they will have 100 virgins when they die—will experience that in the stage of death when you said people get what they expect?
>
> God: *Yes, Angela. If 100 virgins are what they expect, then 100 virgins are what they get. But 100 virgins are not necessarily able to be used in the way they expect. Friendly souls volunteer to be helpful to people in life, as in the little soul story. Also there are friendly souls who will be the 100 virgins for those people who desire them. In the later stages of death, those people realise what they really desired was not really 100 virgins, but a lot of love, which*

they thought 100 virgins could provide. What they soon realise, is that they didn't need 100 virgins to find love. For love is all around them. Love is them. Love is also those people they may have killed along with themselves. They realise their lives on Earth held the same love as they have found in the afterlife; that they could have had the same love in the physical life; that their physical life was indeed surrounded by the same love as surrounds them in the afterlife. If only they had realised, they could have had it all, and physical life as well.

Angela: Is there some way, God, to let those people who are not aware of this love, of your love that surrounds them, to let them know about it?

God: *Yes, Angela, you are doing it with this book. You are being a beacon of love and light. Your light shines out onto the love that surrounds you, and others may then see it as well. Have faith in your ability to shine your light on the love that surrounds you, and all will be well.*

Angela: Thank you, God. I love you.

God: *I know, Angela, and I love you. Angela, you are a beacon of love and light. Your book shines out on all the world. Your love shines out on all the world, when you send it out as love, peace, healing, and joy, to all the people, creatures and the Earth itself. Be a beacon of love and light, and all the world benefits from that. Go now and be that beacon.*

Hitler

Angela: God, I wanted to ask about Hitler.

God: *Angela, no one is ever judged by God or themselves in the afterlife. They merely have a chance to review their life, and decide how they may have done things differently, given their time over again. Hitler has decided to stay in the merged state for a long period. It is here that he can heal from the scars left in his wake, scars for himself and those whose lives he touched. Remember, there are no victims or villains in any life, but having been the Friendly Soul [as we learned about in the Little Soul story] to so many people is a hard thing to recover from. It does take time, as you know it, to do that. Yes, everything is instantaneous, but in your experience it would be years, that he had merged with the all.*

Angela: That is hard to fathom, when everything happens now. How can it take years, as well as it being now?

God: *As you have read in the book* Home with God[21], *the space/time continuum, or Applorange, as the metaphor we have used, represents the now, but your journey through it appears to you to be over eons. The developments you notice on the Earth, although they are all there now in different experiences of the Applorange, you experience them as many years. Hitler experiences the long period you would perceive as a mere instant when he is merged with the one, with the all, and able to reemerge to the spiritual realm. And this is all his choice, so freedom of choice, free will still applies to him. Eternal life still applies to him. As you can see, some of these concepts are hard to reconcile when you are looking from your Earthly human perspective. But the reasons for the book* Home with God *were so you can understand the meaning of life. So you can really give meaning to your life, and your so-called death.*

Angela: I don't really understand the point of trying to save the Earth and its inhabitants from destruction, if it is all just a dream, none of it is real, and we can go back and change things, like our deaths. What's the point?

God: *The point is that you are there to remember who you really are, and having remembered, to remind others of that. You are right that all of life is an illusion, but you are not an illusion, and I am not an illusion. Your love and my love are not illusions. Your love for yourself and others, and for me, for that matter, is what makes you want to change the Earth to a more pleasant one for all concerned.*

Love is the key to all life, and the answer to all questions. Your love is what you are trying to experience, as you seek to experience who you really are. For who you really are is an all-loving being, a being who cares about the experience of yourself and others. You want to spare yourself and others unnecessary pain, and this is why you bother to do what you can to change the world, and to be who and what you really are—a loving creative being. You are a child of God, and God is all loving. That is what you strive to experience in all its many forms. This is why it is worth it.

What is God?

Angela: God, I wanted to ask you about something I read in *Home with God*: "Without you, my power is not made manifest."[21] This started me thinking on the nature of God. I understand that you are experiencing yourself through all of your creation, but I wondered if God has a being outside of your creation. You experience what all of your creation experiences, but do you have experiences, emotions, feelings, thoughts, apart from your creation? If not, then where do these communications come from?

God: *That is a very good question, Angela. The answer is a difficult one for you to grasp. God is all things. God is everything. As you have said, I experience myself through all of my creation, but I am more than my creation. I am an entity of which you cannot fully comprehend. My thoughts are easily sent to you because we are all one, but God is more than the sum of the parts. God is the nothing and the everything. God has an identity of its own, which is more than the individuations added together.*

Angela: So there is more to the ocean, than just the waves clumped together?

God: *Yes, Angela. We are all one. You are part of this great ocean, but the ocean has other parts to it, other than the waves. The ocean includes all of the swimming creatures, the grasses, the boats floating upon it. The ocean analogy is not really holding water, when trying to point out the differences. As I have said in* Home with God[21]*, we are different, but not divided. You are part of God, and I am part of you, but God exists with or without its creation. We are all one, but we are different. God is more than the sum of its parts, as indeed you are.*

Angela learned more from God the following day.

God: *Angela, how are you? How was your day?*

Angela: Wonderful, God. Thanks. How was yours?

God: *My days are filled with joy, always.*

Angela: That's good. But if you feel what all humans feel, your days must be filled with pain as well.

God: *Yes, Angela. That is so. But we are working to change that here and now, with your book, and others like it. We are working to try to let everyone know that they need no longer suffer pain. They can have constant joy, for joy is what they are, and as you discovered recently, they just have to let their joy out. And we know that to experience joy yourself, the best way is to release the joy in another. With everyone taking a small step to release the joy in another, the world could very quickly be filled with the joy that it truly is. It could experience the joy that it truly is.*

Later that day, Angela thought about all she had learned. She finished reading *Home with God* and now felt like she had crossed a line, reached the top of a mountain, and was ready to explore new ideas. She realised there may be more mountains to climb, but she felt like she could at least see where she was going—wherever God leads her. Her heart's desire was that Bill would be beside her throughout her journey.

Spiritual School

God: *Angela, I wondered if we can carry on our conversation about life after death. I wanted to tell you that once you cross over to the other side of the Applorange, there are more lessons for you.*

Angela: You mean for everyone, not just me?

God: *No, Angela, for everyone. You go to a sort of school, where you are educated in the way to be more loving, and be more God-like. You learn how to be more of what you know you are, because in the other side of the Applorange, you are all fully aware of who you are—a child of God. You all have varying degrees of knowledge of how to be that. The school allows you all to know how to be the best you can be, in your various stages of development. Once you learn about a specific aspect of divinity, you can choose to learn about more aspects of divinity, or to return to the physical plane—the apple in our metaphor, and practise what you have learned.*

With the help of your teachers, you map out a plan—a rough plan, of what you want to achieve, and how. You then collaborate with others to help them achieve what they need to achieve, and they or others do the same for you. Once you have decided what you want to achieve, and you decide who are going to help you achieve your goals, you return to the physical plane. You are born to parents you have selected, with the help of your guides, and voila— you are born back into the physical world, where you practise what you have learned.

Sometimes, in order for you to achieve your goals of practising your divinity, or helping others practise theirs, it is necessary to forget who you are, but once you have achieved your goals as a forgetful person, you are then able to remember who you are, and wake up. There may still be more lessons for you once you have woken up, as you have found, but once you have woken up, you are then able to help others to wake up, as well. Some are ready to wake up, and will not take much reminding of who they are. Others are not yet ready, because they haven't yet achieved their aims. But you are there to help each other achieve your goals, and help each other remember who you are. Did you have any questions?

Angela: I am a bit confused about how we are all here to wake each other up—to remind each other of who we are. It seems those who have been in the physical plane for longer should be more aware of who they are, because they have been exposed to more attempts to wake them up for longer, but I don't see a lot of evidence of that. And what then is the role of the indigo and crystal children?

God: *You are right, Angela. Because of the way that the world is heading, it has been decided that we need to try to have as many people awake now as possible. The indigo and crystal children are more aware of who they are from an early age, so don't take a lot of reminding, whereas some of your older citizens take a bit more reminding.*

Remember, too, everyone is in various stages of development. Some are working on much more basic aspects of divinity, whereas others are tackling harder lessons.

Angela: So, some need to complete more goals of helping others and such, before they can awaken, whereas others are just sleeping more soundly. Is that correct?

God: *Yes, Angela. If you ask your higher self during meditation, you can know which category a person falls into.*

Angela: If we on Earth become all fully awake, I assume we would be more loving because we know we are all one. If we are all in various stages of development, however, I assume there will still be some who are more loving than others. If everyone is awake, would there be no more violent crime, or do some of us still require more lessons, as I did, once we are awake, before we can all live happily together, or will we need to take those small brave steps first, before we can live in peace, if we are all awake?

God: *Well, Angela, that is really a couple of questions in one, but I understand what you're asking is "What will the world be like, if everyone were to wake up?" And yes, everyone would know they are children of God, and God is love, and therefore, they themselves are love. But as you have gone through a process over the last three or so years to get to where you are today, others will have processes they will need to go through before they can live in peace. Some people have a lot of people to forgive before they can live in peace, and many issues they need to put to rest. It is not an instantaneous thing, but a process that started the moment each person asks: "Who am I? And what am I doing here?"*

Were they all your questions, Angela?

Angela: I wondered, once we are awake, as well as remembering who we are, why we don't also remember other things, like what it's like in the spiritual realm. You have piqued my curiosity with your talk of schools. I wondered what these schools would be like, and why is the other side such a mystery. Is it just too different to be comprehensible?

God: *That's right, Angela. You would have difficulty getting your head around what it's like in spirit, as you did when we were talking about simultaneous sequential occurrences. As you were just thinking, in the New Spirituality, there will be greater communications between the physical and the spiritual realm, so you will come to know a bit more about the other side, but just as you needed more information before being comfortable with this message, you would require a bit more information before you were comfortable with that information, as well.*

Angela, you can know your life is a series of lessons. Even your life in the spiritual plane is filled with lessons. Some lessons have prerequisites, just like Psychology 201 may require you to have done Psychology 101. You had to have some information before you were ready to receive this information. You receive some of that while you sleep.

Angela: God, I wanted to ask you about the dream I had, that felt like I was in class. I wondered if it was a class I was in during my sleep, as you had been telling me about, or just a dream.

God: *Angela, there is no such thing as "just a dream". Every dream has a purpose, not always a serious purpose, but always there is a purpose. Usually your subconscious gets something from the dream, which it stores away for later use. This was the case with your dream last night.*

The dream last night was, indeed, a class you attended. You were learning about the way problems children have can be magnified, if they are not dealt with at the time. They can easily become compounded, and then end up being more difficult to release. It is therefore best to catch any problem when a child is young. The problem is that a lot of the problems children have are actually caused by their parents.

Children are like giant sponges. They soak up, not only knowledge, but also attitudes to all manner of things on the Earth, and in society. It is much better to allow children to form their own attitudes to the things they encounter, but this takes a fair bit of restraint and careful consideration on behalf of their parents.

As you learned from Tomorrow's God[22] [by Neale Donald Walsch], *the New Spirituality will focus on allowing children to do just that, within the framework of teaching them the three Rs, which, if you remember were Reconciliation, Re-creation, and Reunification.*

Although Angela and Bill had never had children of their own, they had nieces and nephews, and great-nieces and great-nephews, so Angela hoped her lesson about children being sponges may be of some benefit to them. If not, she knew she could teach what she had learned through her book, and hopefully help many more parents to understand their responsibility in shaping their children's views on life.

> God: *Angela, I wanted to let your readers know there is some information they need to wait for. It is not that they can't accept that information yet, but they need other information first. Perhaps if they are thinking there are some parts of the book that don't make sense now, they should leave it for a while, and come back to it later, as you have just done with* The Lightworker's Way[23], *by Doreen Virtue, Ph.D.*
>
> Angela: Was that also the case when I read *Conversations With God*[15] many years ago?
>
> God: *Yes, Angela. That is right. Everything happens at the best possible time for you.*
>
> Angela: I wondered if I really should have woken up all those years ago, when I bought *Conversations With God* or my Angel Tarot cards. But then I remembered what the Light Being told me, that I needed everything that has happened to me, to get to where I am today.
>
> God: *That's right, Angela. There have been lessons all along your path to date. Now that you are awake, you are more aware of your lessons, and are consciously aiming to apply your lessons, but you had lessons before you woke up. You just weren't aware what they were. You learned from them nonetheless.*

Light Being Advice

God's comments reminded Angela of the conversation she had, after starting to read *The Light Workers Way*[23]. She put the book down to start her evening meditation. She asked to speak to guides of the highest vibration as usual and was elated with the greeting she received.

"Love to you, Angela."

Angela knew immediately this was not her normal guides. She felt as though heaven had rained all of its love down on her. Somehow she knew this being.

Angela: Love to you Being of Light. What name can I give you?

"Light Being is a good name."

Angela: Can you please answer my questions?

Light Being: *Surely, Angela.*

Angela: Why did I suffer depression earlier in my life, if I am a lightworker designed to not suffer the fear that holds down the planet?

Light Being: *Angela, your path was chosen before you incarnated. Your past has made you the person you are today. Those lessons of the past were necessary to get you to where you are now.*

Angela: Why, if there is such urgency, did my mission start so late in life?

Light Being: *Again, all was necessary. You do not recognise the stepping stones creating your path to your current place, but they were necessary nonetheless.*

Angela: If everyone has guides to help them, how did we get to such a bad situation in the environment? Where did the inspiration for these inventions come from?

Light Being: *Angela, you can know that not all the plastics and chemicals that have caused harm are bad in and of themselves. There is a time and place for everything. However, humans have used these things in ways that they were not intended. Please educate them of their folly.*

Angela: I don't feel qualified to preach to people too much about environmental damage. I, too, have polluted and used plastics, not recycled, and basically taken the easiest path.

Light Being: *Give your mistakes to heaven as you have learned from the fairies and Doreen Virtue Ph.D. But you are as qualified as the next person to educate others about the right way to treat the environment. Please start with your concern for turtles and work from there. Remember to pick up your rubbish, don't pollute with harmful chemicals, recycle, treat plants and animals with respect, and love all of life, including yourself. Be a voice of love and caring for the Earth and all of its creatures. Be at peace. Don't forget to have fun.*

Angela: That's easier said than done.

Light Being: *Love is the key. Be at peace.*

Angela: Thank you Light Being for your love and assistance.

Despite her feeling guilty for not being a very good friend to the Earth, following her conversation with the Light Being, Angela felt an overwhelming love and great joy. This being, to whom she had just spoken, had certainly touched her heart and made it swell with love. Angela felt privileged to receive this loving communication, and was beginning to feel special. She was quickly reminded she was supposed to have a swelled heart, not a swelled head, and that everyone is special. She took the Light Being's advice and sent her mistakes to heaven as she had learned from another of Doreen Virtue's books, *Healing With The Fairies*[18].

At the time of her original reading, Angela had found some parts of *The Lightworker's Way*[23] really didn't make sense to her, and yet when she reread it some time later, she couldn't remember what the problem had been. She knew her mind was like a sponge, absorbing so much information, but it seemed to be selective about what it accepted to absorb. As seemed to always be the case, God provided clarification.

Wisdom of the Higher Self

Angela: God, you were going to clarify what we were talking about in relation to our higher selves having all the knowledge we ever need.

God: *Yes, Angela. Your higher self already knows everything you will ever come to know in this lifetime, but for you to experience this knowledge in your physical existence, you have to take this information into your brain. To do this, you need to have this information inserted there by means of your senses, through books, by hearing it, seeing it, reading it, etc.*

Angela: What about the lessons you said we have while we sleep?

God: *Yes, Angela, those lessons still use your physical senses, but not the ones you know about.*

Angela: What senses don't I know about?

God: *Those senses which take information direct from another being and implant it into your subconscious.*

Angela: Couldn't our higher selves do that, then?

God: *Angela, there are many things of which you are not aware, and I could explain them all to you here, but it would be a very long book. Suffice to say, your higher self communicates with the physical you through your emotions, and through meditation, but the knowledge which it has can only be transmitted into your brain through another means, another sense.*

Angela: You said we should remember that our higher selves have all the knowledge we will ever need, and the greatest wisdom comes from our higher selves. Is it that we take information into our brains from outside sources, but it is the wisdom of our higher selves which causes this information to resonate within us so we know it to be truth? And this is where the feeling comes in?

God: *That's right, Angela.*

Angela: How do you account for people accepting information as truth, when it clearly isn't, like the "London bombing" conspiracy theories I have just been watching on *4 Corners*[24]?

God: *Well, Angela, there are many reasons people accept untruth as truth. Usually it involves fear. In the case of the Muslims who wish to believe it is not possible that there are people within their religion who would kill innocent civilians, it is less fearful to believe the government lies to them, when they already have evidence of that, with weapons of mass destruction that didn't exist and such, than it is to believe that their sweet and wonderful religion, which has given them such strength, can cause others to kill themselves and many others. If they were to listen to their higher selves, they would learn the truth of the situation, and if they listened to and accepted the feelings they get when they hear about these conspiracy theories, in conjunction with thinking love, they would come to understand the truth.*

The truth is that no religion, theory, sect, or group which wishes to divide people from each other can offer the complete truth for any person. For, as you have learned, we are all one. All people are united by God's love, by my love. This is the truth your higher self would reveal to you, if you let it.

Angela: God, you were saying we need books and teachers to implant the information, but is that only if we don't meditate? If we meditate, can we not get the information directly from our higher selves?

God: *That's right, Angela.*

Angela: So the more we meditate, the wiser we would be, or the more knowledgeable, at least?

God: *Yes, Angela, but your higher self will only give you information as you need it, and as you ask for it. You can't download all of your higher self's knowledge in one extra-long meditation session.*

Angela: Ok, God. Now, you said that we have senses in our brain, which implant information directly from another being into our subconscious. That sounds a bit scary. Which other beings have access to these senses?

God: *Angela, there is nothing to fear. Only those beings, which you have given permission to, can do this. These beings are normally teachers in the spirit realm, or ascended masters realm, who are helping you with your lessons here in the physical realm.*

Angela: If our higher selves have all of the knowledge we will ever need, why don't these lessons come from our higher selves?

God: *Good question, Angela. Your higher self has the knowledge, but that knowledge is more easily imparted to your brain from another being, than from your higher self. Your higher self is available for acquiring information through meditation and your feelings, but is not the best source of information to impart information direct to your subconscious.*

As you have learned, you have many helpers, many teachers who will be able to impart information to you in just the right way to make it useful to you. But remember too, though there are many beings, we are all one. The information easily passes from one to another.

Simultaneous and Sequential

One night after experiencing Jesus' healing help, Angela asked if he wanted to talk to her.

Jesus: *Yes, Angela, I did. I wanted to tell you how much I love you. It is not only God who appreciates the love you have given. I also appreciate your love. But, I too, love all the people of the world. Angela, you are a joy to help, a joy to heal. Your love is returned to me. My love and your love combine to make real magic. Love is truly a magical thing. It is as wonderful an experience for me as it is for you. I appreciate the chance to help you, and to share your love.*

Angela: Jesus, I am not sure if you are able to answer this in a way I will understand, but I wondered how you can communicate with, and heal multiple people at the one time. I understand there is really only the now for you, but you are communicating with me in my time zone, so to speak, and presumably others in their time zones, but all of these time zones are all at once for you, so you are a busy boy/spirit.

Jesus: *Yes, Angela. You are right that this all happens instantly for me, but it is as God explained in the book* Home with God: *everything happens simultaneously, but sequentially, as well. You cannot comprehend that from your perspective on Earth, but suffice to say, it is easy for me to have communications with more than one person at different places, and different times in this instant that I experience.*

Angela was grateful for the information she received from her teachers. She knew that all of her life held lessons if she looked for them. Still, she never expected to find so many valuable lessons in a trip to a casino.

Gambling Lessons

The Test

Angela and her sister, Beth, had planned a girls' long weekend away at a coastal resort and casino. Beth was an avid poker machine player, and Angela normally enjoyed it as well. Angela looked forward to recapturing some of the closeness in their relationship which had escaped them in recent years.

The day before they were due to leave, Angela woke early. Whilst lying in bed wondering whether to try to go back to sleep, or get up and start her day, she felt God was calling her to talk to him.

> God: *Angela, I wanted to let you know you can be confident in your abilities to hear my messages. You don't need a formal meeting to do that, but I requested a formal meeting this morning because I wanted to tell you that you can go ahead and print out your book now. The lessons phase of your book is nearing an end, and you were hoping for Bill to read it first. This weekend would be a good opportunity for him.*

Angela: It's a bit scary for me, God.

God: *I know you fear his reactions. But you know he has mellowed a lot lately. His angels and guides have been working with him too, even though he is not aware of it. You might be pleasantly surprised.*

As it was her last day before her long weekend, Angela had a busy day. There were a couple of staff away and Angela covered reception. As well as all the things she needed to do for work, she had to find some time to print out the hundreds of pages of her manuscript.

As the day progressed, it seemed everyone picked that day to want everything done. Payments needed to be made and invoices sent. It was also staff payday, but there was a problem with the accounting software and it took her twice as long as normal to process the payments. As she tried to complete her tasks, more were added and the stress compounded. She started to become overwrought. Angela knew she should be able to let love see her through difficult and stressful times like this, but she wasn't thinking love, she was thinking panic.

One of her tasks was to walk up the street to the nearby supermarket to buy a bottle of distilled water urgently required in the factory. Someone had forgotten to order it from the regular supplier. As she waited in the checkout queue, she anxiously watched the minutes tick away on her wristwatch. She suddenly realised she wouldn't make it back to the office in time to prepare the dispatch documents for goods required to ship that day. Despite a strong urge to sit down in the supermarket aisle and have a nervous breakdown, she asked her angels for help. She called the office on her mobile phone, requesting assistance from a colleague to prepare the documents.

From that moment on, she felt better and managed to complete all of her assigned tasks, including the printing.

It was late in the day before she realised she had been tested on the lessons she had learned, and she felt like a hopeless failure.

She spoke to Jesus that evening.

> Jesus: *Angela, I wanted to talk to you because I know you feel bad because you failed your test.*
>
> Angela: Yes, Jesus. I feel that I have let you and God down, because I wasn't able to apply my lessons when it counted.
>
> Jesus: *No, Angela, you didn't do too well. But these things take time. As with living in the moment, awareness is a major step. You did become aware of your reactions and started to work to change them, but in the beginning you did fail to apply your lessons. You know now you could have thought love, and not worried about the time slipping away. You know you can live in the moment, even when you have a heavy schedule, and people are demanding various things be done straight away. You just became*

overwhelmed. You will do better next time, and then better again the time after that.

Angela: Jesus, I know I didn't do well, but thinking back, with lots of time constraints, I am not sure how I would have coped better given my time over again.

Jesus: *Yes, Angela. You could have. You would have thought 'love' more. This would have left you calmer. You built from one stressful moment to the next. If you had thought love in each of those moments, the stress would not have built up, and you would have coped much better. Love is the key. You forgot that in the beginning.*

Angela: Yes, Jesus. I will do better next time. Thanks, Jesus, for your help.

Jesus: *You're welcome, Angela. I love you, and want only the best for you and the rest of humanity. You have experienced the difficulty everyone faces in times of stress—if you allow it, it will escalate, and you cannot cope. It was only when you started thinking love and asking for help, that you started winding down your stress levels. Remember to think love before all that you do, and you cannot fail.*

Angela: When you have so many other things to think about, with so many things to be done, it is hard to think love as well.

Jesus: *Angela, you know you can plan your day, your hour, your minute, and then only think of one thing—the thing you need to in that moment, but before you think about that thing, think love, and everything will run much more smoothly.*

Angela: Jesus, I will try to remember in future. Can you please remind me?

Jesus: *Yes, Angela, I can. Have no fear, you can only improve. Remember what God has told you: everyone is evolving; everyone is doing the best they can in any situation, but you are all evolving—all improving—every day. You may have a few setbacks, but the overall path is always up.*

Angela spoke to God the next morning, prior to leaving for her trip.

Angela: Hello, God. I am afraid I let you down yesterday.

God: *No, Angela. You let yourself down, but you have nothing to prove to me—ever. I love you just as you are, warts and all. I love you because you are you, whether or not you achieve your aims of thinking love in all that you do, which you didn't quite manage yesterday. But as Jesus told you, next time you'll do a little better, and the time after that, a little better still. Have faith, have love, and all will be well. Remember in the future, that if you think love before tackling any difficulties, the difficulties will disappear, and everything is made easy.*

Angela: I will try to remember, God, and have asked for help with this.

God: *Yes, Angela, you have many who can help you. As you found out yesterday, when you remembered to ask for help, you found help from angels and your workmates. Remember too, in future, help is always available.*

Angela: I will try to remember, God.

God: *Remember to love yourself first, in all that you do, and then you have love to share with others. Remember that love is the key to all problems, all situations.*

Angela: Ok, God. I will think positive about this, as well, in future. From now on, I will think love before all that I do. I will love myself first, and then love others, and my life will be easy from this point forward.

God: *Sounds good, Angela. You may have setbacks, but if you intend to be a certain way then chances are this is how you will be. Good luck.*

Angela: Thanks, God. Will you wish me good luck at the casino, too?

God: *Yes, Angela. I wish for you the luck that you choose for yourself. If winning is your desire, then I wish you that.*

Angela: I had a talk with my higher self, and decided that small wins would be ok.

God: *Ok, Angela, have a wonderful time and remember that you take me with you wherever you go.*

Bill watched as Angela packed the last of her things in her overnight bag. At the last minute, she decided to pack some jewelry in a small jewelry case, a gift from a friend for a healing. In there was a special topaz pendant Bill had bought for her during an overseas trip.

"Don't lose it," he said, as he kissed her goodbye.

Love for Poker Machines

After arriving at the casino, Beth and Angela soon settled in to playing the poker machines. The next day, after a tiring shopping expedition, while her sister played on the machines, Angela went upstairs for a rest. She took the opportunity to do a little meditation, including a healing on herself, loving the world, and a conversation with God.

God: *Angela, you can take heart from the fact that love will prevail in any situation, even when playing the pokies. Love yourself first in that situation, love the machine you are playing, and those who benefit from your money, and all will be well. Remember that love is the key to all situations, even poker machine playing.*

Love yourself and all the world, and you cannot fail. Love yourself and all those around you, and you must succeed. Love yourself first, and then others, and all will be well. You are a child of God, and can create your own reality. Remember you can choose the outcome you desire. Have faith, and all will be well.

Gambling Rules Your Life

That evening, Angela and Beth went to a show and it was nearly midnight when they went to the casino to gamble. Angela tried to put into practice what God had told her earlier: she thought love for herself, the machine, and all those who benefited from her money. She was amazed to find that loving the machine she was playing seemed to have an effect. She started to win instead of losing. She wasn't winning large amounts, but she did start to recoup some of the money she had previously lost.

She had intended to just play for a little while and then go to bed, but found herself hoping for another win, a bigger win, and before she knew it, it was after 1.00 am. She hadn't actually managed her afternoon nap, and she wasn't used to such late nights. She was just about asleep on her feet.

The next morning, they made sure they rose in time to eat a sumptuous breakfast, and allow another hour playing the pokies before checkout time. Angela asked God if he could help her to win a jackpot, and he said that he could. Angela did manage to win a mini-jackpot of about $20, but she was aiming for the $11,000 jackpot, so continued to play right up to checkout time. She continued to win small amounts and came away with about what she started with.

Beth had run out of money earlier, and had gone up to the room to pack. When Angela arrived at their room, Beth had all the bags ready to go. Angela thought she finished packing her things before going to breakfast, so she just had to grab everything and go.

On the drive home, Angela had an awful feeling she forgot to pack her little jewelry case. When Angela arrived home, she frantically unpacked her bag. The jewelry case was not there. She was devastated. When she rang Beth to ask if she checked the drawer which it had been in, Beth said she had checked all but that one.

"I can't believe it!" Angela exclaimed as she hung up the phone. "How could I be so obsessed with playing poker machines and trying to win money that I allowed it to take priority over packing of my things?" Looking back, it seemed the poker machines had momentarily ruled her life.

She rang the hotel and waited a long couple of hours before they returned her call.

Luckily, they located the jewelry case, and it was returned the next day.

"If I never play on a poker machine again, it will be too soon," she told Bill, as she carefully placed her topaz pendant back in her jewelry box.

The Lessons

After Angela recovered from losing her jewelry case, and losing her perspective on gambling, she asked Bill if he had read her book and what he thought of it. She could hear her heart pounding in her chest as she waited for him to answer.

"I'll tell you in more detail later, but if you really want to know, I think you're a wanker."

"But you still love me though?"

"Yes, I still love you."

She spoke to Jesus the next day.

> Jesus: *Angela, I wanted to tell you that all will be well. You have fear that things will not be right between you and Bill, now that he has read most of your book. But remember he still loves you, despite the things he told you about how he felt about your book. You know his angels and guides are helping him, just as yours are helping you. He has his own aims he wishes to achieve in his life, and yours and his aims need not be mutually exclusive, even though they may appear to be. Do not fear. Remember your resolve to not let the opinions of others deter you from your aims. That includes the opinions of Bill.*
>
> Angela: It is easy to dismiss others' opinions when they are not your close loved ones.
>
> Jesus: *I know it makes it more difficult, Angela. But have faith in yourself. Have faith in your abilities, and you can achieve all of your aims, and your love can still thrive.*

After loving the world, Angela spoke to God.

God: *Angela, I wanted to ask you what lessons you learned during your weekend away.*

Angela: I learned a lot, God. I learned there is a fine line between enjoyment and obsession, when it comes to gambling. I learned love helps even when you're gambling. I learned to listen to my body when it is telling me that it is time for bed, for I really regretted the consequences from the lack of sleep that resulted from not heeding my body's call.

God: *Yes, Angela. Those are all wonderful lessons, but you know what the greatest lesson was?*

Angela: What, God?

God: *The greatest lesson was that you can find a way to love yourself and the world no matter where you go or what you do. You can also talk to God no matter where you go or what you do. And I did help you win a jackpot, not the jackpot you were hoping for, but I didn't say which jackpot I would help you win.*

Angela: No, you didn't God, and thank you.

God: *You're welcome, Angela. You are right. There is a fine line between enjoyment and obsession. It is usually caused by greed. Getting back the money you lost just doesn't seem enough; you have to try to get more and more.*

Angela: I guess that is the fun of it, as well. There is always a chance to win big.

God: *There is always a chance you will lose it all, as well. While you play for enjoyment, you are likely to succeed. If you play for greed, chances are you will fail. Greed is only necessary when you don't have sufficient faith in the universe to bring you all of your desires. There is no need to try to break the bank, because the universe will bring you whatever you desire, if you believe it so, and if it is your will.*

Angela: Ok, God. Greed did rear its ugly head quite a few times on the weekend, and I can see now that greed is what causes obsession, that and not trusting the universe and our creative abilities. Were there any other messages, God?

God: *Yes, Angela. I wanted to tell you all will be well with Bill. Have no fear. I know you are afraid of his reaction to your book, but you said yourself that he still loves you, even if he thinks 'you're a wanker'. You know that here, too, the universe is bringing you all of your desires. Even though you think your and his desires are mutually exclusive, remember the story of tying up your camel. The universe must find a way to get you home if you desire that, and it must also find a way to let your camel be free to roam, if that is its desire. The universe must find a way to achieve both of your desires. Have no fear. All will be well.*

Angela: Ok, God. I will trust in the universe to bring me all of my desires, and know that both Bill and I can be happy.

God: *That's right, Angela. You can create your own reality. Remember, you are a child of God, and can create whatever you desire. Have faith and all will be well. Go now and enjoy your evening. We will talk again tomorrow evening, or whenever you next wish to, but remember you can talk to me any time, night or day. I am with you always.*

Angela was beginning to have faith that God could be right about Bill. There wasn't much evidence of it yet, but Angela hoped her faith would pay off.

Lessons of Faith and Love

Overcoming Fear

Love and faith were the cornerstones of all the lessons Angela received. She had been told that, because we are all one, information passed easily between beings. She knew love, too, was passed between beings. She had felt such love emanating from her angels, guides, Mother Earth, Jesus, and God. She began to wish she could receive faith in the same manner. But Angela knew faith was one thing she would have to find within herself.

> Jesus: *Angela, you can know your life is taking off now. You have learned your lessons well. You are beginning to understand how to watch your thoughts and not be drawn into the identity of your ego. As Allan explained, practice makes perfect. Have faith in your abilities. Have faith in us.*
>
> *Remember to love yourself before sending your love out into the world. You are now finding the joy that resides within your heart. That joy is your love experienced.*

There seemed to be a pause in Jesus' words, which Angela came to believe meant she had started to let her thoughts interfere with the message she was hearing.

Jesus then resumed: *You can know our messages can come to you loud and clear. Have faith in yourself and all will be well.*

Angela: Ok, Jesus. I have faith your messages can be heard by me as loud and clear.

Jesus: *Do not doubt your abilities, Angela. Think love. Then listen. Remember to love yourself before sending your love out into the world. Be the beacon you know you can be.*

You are a beacon of love and light as you raise your vibration and send your love out into the world. You are a beacon of love and light as you write our words and yours in your book. You are a beacon of love and light to all you meet, and to all you think of with love. Have faith in your abilities to heal the world as you send your love, peace and healing out into the world, as you spread the word in your book, and as you speak to and think about others with love.

Be not afraid of any situation that arises. You have all the tools you need to survive any situation, to overcome any challenges. You have the love of God dwelling within you. Love is all you need to get by. Your love, God's love is always with you, in any situation. You can rely on that love always.

Angela: Why do we all have difficulties in trusting our abilities?

Jesus: *Your culture has instilled fear in you from when you were a baby. Instead of giving you the confidence to meet any challenge and overcome every obstacle, your culture, starting with your parents, instilled fear from an early age.*

Educate the parents of the world to allow their children to encounter the beauty and wonder of the world, without fear. They can teach their children about ways to trust in their abilities as creative beings, whilst still protecting them from danger. You can teach your children to look both ways when crossing the road, without them being afraid of being run over.

All of life holds risks. It is possible to make your children aware of the risks, without making them afraid of them. Teach your children they can move mountains, and their faith will be rewarded. Love and faith are the two keys to overcoming fear. Have love for yourself; have faith in yourself, and you cannot fail.

Whose Love?

After all of her lessons about having faith, about living in the moment, about thinking love, and sending love out into the world, Angela began to be happy.

Although she still had difficulties, she started to realise she could use all of these tools to overcome her difficulties, and even cherish them. She was, indeed, becoming God's confident, faithful, invincible beacon.

While she had God's love, she could do anything. She wasn't quite up to the stage of walking on water, but she felt like she was getting closer every day she had God's love.

God: *Angela, I wanted to talk to you, to tell you again how much I love you. I love you so much more than you can imagine. I love you so much more than words can say. My love is so great, it overwhelms you. My love is so great, it bathes you in honey, and allows you to breathe in that honey through every pore of your skin. My love is so great, you cannot know the full extent of my love for you, and all of my creation. Please take a moment to feel some of my wondrous love.*

...

Angela: Thanks, God. I felt like I was wrapped in the arms of love. The trouble is, God, once one feels love enveloping one like that, one doesn't want to leave that feeling. I am tempted to sit and dwell in it all day.

God: *I know it is tempting, Angela, but you don't need to sit and dwell in it. You can experience that same love as you go about your daily activities. Ask and you shall receive.*

Angela: Ok, God. I would like to feel that love from time to time throughout my day, every day.

God: *Your wish is my command.*

The next day was a Monday, and true to his word, God visited Angela with demonstrations of his love, a number of times throughout her working day.

After loving the world that evening, she spoke to God about it.

> God: *Angela, you are a joy to me. The love you send out to all the world reaches me at every point, for we are all one. As you love the world, you love me, and I really appreciate your love.*
>
> Angela: And I really appreciate your love, God, and Jesus' love, and Mother Earth's love.
>
> God: *You're welcome, Angela, on behalf of those you mentioned. But the love you send out is returned from all quarters. You can feel it now through your body. Your love, my love, our love is truly magical.*
>
> Angela: God, I felt your love off and on throughout the day. I felt an increased vibration, and a smooth silky feeling in my body. I assumed it was you, and when I asked if it was you, I got a yes, so I guess it was.
>
> God: *Yes, Angela. You still are not convinced that when you talk to God, you get an answer from God.*
>
> Angela: Well, I am convinced it could be from you, but I sometimes wonder if it could be coming from my mind.

God: *Yes, Angela, the answer could be coming from your mind, but it wasn't. It was me, God—the one who loves you more than words can say, the one who wants to demonstrate my love to you, the one who loves you now and always. That one.*

Angela: Ok, God. You seem to be getting a bit offended.

God: *You know that nothing you can do can ever offend me. My love is unconditional, but you know you can have more faith in your ability to hear my voice throughout the day. Remember if you think love before you talk to me, then chances are the answer is coming from me. And you know you couldn't help but think love when you were asking if the love you felt was coming from me, because you were feeling love.*

Angela: Yes, God, and I do appreciate it. It was a bit distracting, but definitely worth it. You left me feeling like skipping around the office.

God: *I know, Angela. I was there. I am part of you, and all of my creation. I experience all you experience, and I feel my love, and your love.*

Angela: Thanks, God. I wouldn't mind carrying on with this every day, and see how I go.

God: *Ok, Angela. Your wish is my command.*

The next evening, Angela spoke to God again.

Angela: You didn't send me your love today.

God: *No, Angela. You know why, don't you?*

Angela: I think so, God, but you tell me.

God: *Because I wanted you to realise that you don't need my love, God's love, from any external source. Your love, your internal source of love, is all you will ever need. You found out when you were walking up the street: you felt love for me, for yourself, and all of my creation, because you realised we are all one, and it is my love within you that you feel whenever you call upon love.*

My love is your love is our love. You have all the love you will ever need to get by. You know love is all around you, but love is within you. You are pure love. You know you can feel your love whenever you desire.

Angela: Yes, that is what I deduced was my lesson for today, and I think I remarked to you that it was a sneaky thing to do.

God: *It was a bit, wasn't it? But you learned the lesson well. You can call on me at any time for help, or that little bit of extra love to get you through, if you want to go skipping around the office. But remember you can achieve the same results without my help, without the extra love. You have sufficient for all your needs.*

Believe and it is So

There were many lessons on many days.

> God: *Angela, you know that it is really me you're talking to, right?*

Angela: I guess.

> God: *You were having trouble before, because you couldn't differentiate between your own thoughts, and my answers.*

Angela: That's right, God. When I am talking to you like this with notebook in hand, it seems easier for me to stop my thoughts, and let you talk. But when I am just asking a question in the middle of doing something, I am not sure whether it is me or you answering. I did ask: "Is that me or you?" but can I be sure the answer comes from you?

> God: *Yes, Angela, it is a difficult problem, but only because you don't have sufficient faith in your abilities. If you had strong faith in your abilities to hear our messages, you would have strong faith in the messages you get, and strong faith that we would let you know if it is you or us talking.*

Angela: Ok, so how can I fix this?

> God: *Believe, and it is so. If you believe you can discern our messages from your thoughts, that is what will be. Remember, you create your own reality. If you are confident the answers you receive to questions addressed to*

God really come from God, then they will. Lack of faith in the origins of the messages will allow your own mind to place the answers there.

Angela: So, how does one acquire confidence?

God: *Just as in your skiing, confidence comes from practice. You might have a couple of falls from time to time, but pick yourself up and carry on. Believe in your own abilities, and you will get better and better.*

Angela: Ok, God. Thank you.

God: *You're welcome, Angela. Go now and get your dinner, but remember, I love you. Remember, my love is real. Remember, you create your own reality. Remember, love is all there is. Remember, we are all one.*

Angela: That's a lot to remember.

God: *Yes, Angela. As you were asking before, if this is another lesson, as I was saying: "All of life is a lesson, if you choose it to be, if you are paying attention." And you said: "I was afraid of that." You know life was meant to be easy, including all of your lessons. The universe is bringing you all of your desires; you have so much help, both physical and spiritual. Life can be a joy forever, while you are learning your lessons.*

Have faith, have love, and all will be well. Go now, and take my love with you, and have confidence in your abilities to hear my messages, and all will be well.

Building Confidence

Angela and Bill had only taken up skiing in the last few years. Angela knew she was being a beacon with her skiing, as well. Just as with her spiritual endeavours, if she could learn to ski at such a late stage in her life, anyone could. And if anyone could do what she had done— learn to talk to spiritual beings and God—then surely anyone could do anything they set their mind to, including become confident in the spiritual messages they were transcribing.

She still had some difficulties when writing God's words, as her mind would insert a word here or there. God would let her know if there was a problem, otherwise he said the gist of what she wrote was correct. But Angela knew things were getting serious, when she was told Jesus would be giving her exercises in transcribing his messages.

Night after night, Jesus would give her alphabet exercises to transcribe: "A is for aardvark. B is for Bob. L is for Larry." The exercises went on and on, and were very boring for her active mind. Jesus offered the carrot that, once Angela had mastered these lessons, she would learn the name of the publisher of her book.

Some nights Jesus ended the conversation with a name, which Angela later discovered was not a real publisher. Initially, she was devastated as she knew she must have misheard. As it happened again and again, she realised there was no way she could have been so wrong about the publishers name while improving remarkably, according to Jesus, with the other words she was transcribing.

Angela: Hello, Jesus.

Jesus: *Hello Angela. Are you ready to hear the name of your publisher?*

Angela: Of course I am, Jesus. I am a confident person now. I really am feeling a bit more confident, Jesus.

Jesus: *That's good, Angela, because the name of the publisher is Larson.*

Angela: What was it again, Jesus?

Jesus: *Angela, are you sure you want to know the name?*

Angela: Yes, I'm sure.

Jesus: *Well, just write it down again as I tell you the name is Pearson.*

Angela: I'm guessing that's not right.

Jesus: *Why do you say that, Angela?*

Angela: Because of the feeling I have. I'm not feeling joy.

Jesus: *You don't feel joy, because you are frightened of being wrong.*

Angela: Yes.

Jesus: *Well, Angela, you are wrong on this occasion, but you could have been right, if you had more confidence in your abilities.*

Angela: Well, tell me where to turn on the confidence switch, then?

Jesus: *There is no switch, Angela. Practice makes perfect.*

Angela: Practice at what?

Jesus: *Practice at being confident.*

Angela: Normally, I would think that I have to have something to be confident about, before I could practise it. But you want me to be confident before having anything to be confident about.

Jesus: *Yes, Angela, you have hit the nail on the head. You can be confident in your abilities. This will lead to your having a reason to be confident in your abilities, which will lead you to being even more confident in your abilities.*

Angela: So, this is another test of faith, Jesus?

Jesus: *That's right, Angela. You previously learned to have faith in God, faith in the universe to bring you your desires, and faith in the origin of these messages. Now you have to apply your faith to yourself—to have faith in yourself and your abilities—your abilities to hear our messages, and your abilities to create your own reality, in which clear messages are possible.*

Angela: Ok, Jesus, I can do that.

Jesus: *Yes, Angela, I know you can do it. You just have to apply your previous lessons to this current challenge.*

Remember that thinking love always helps you to conquer any challenges.

Angela: Ok, Jesus. Love.

Jesus: *That's the way, Angela. We will try again tomorrow. Go now and love the world. Have no fear. Your confidence is increasing gradually.*

Some years later, Angela read the book, *The Confidence Gap*, by Dr Russ Harris[25]. She was interested to find that he promoted acting confidently, prior to feeling confident, just as Jesus had advised.

With hindsight, after reading *The Confidence Gap*, Angela realised that although the exercises in the book definitely helped her, it was her ability to think love which helped the most. Although the book helped her cope with fear, it was thinking love which helped her overcome fear entirely. She knew that fear would show its face again, but she also knew that God and Jesus were right. She had all of the resources she needed to overcome any difficulties. Back then, however, she hadn't learned to apply those resources.

Angela: Hello, God.

God: *Hello, Angela. How was your day?*

Angela: Ok, God. I didn't think love enough, I know.

God: *No, Angela, but you did ok, which is why you had an ok day.*

Angela: Ok, God.

God: *Angela, I wanted to talk to you about where you go from here.*

Angela: God, at the moment, it feels like I'm not going anywhere anytime soon. I keep having *Groundhog Day* over again.

God: *I know it seems that way, Angela, but you are improving, and your life is improving, as well, but you are too busy focusing on this current lesson to notice.*

Angela: Ok, God, so where am I going from here?

God: *Upwards, Angela, onwards and upwards.*

But Jesus' alphabet exercises seemed to go on and on, and she felt like she was having *Groundhog Day* repeatedly.

Then suddenly, one day, they were finished. There was no publisher's name to learn, and Angela realised that the exercises were just a way to improve her transcription skills and her confidence.

God: *Angela, now that you are confident again, I can tell you a little story.*

Angela: Ok, God, but I'm not that confident.

God: *You will be.*

My story is about a beautiful woman, who had learned a lot of lessons. Some of them were painful lessons, but each lesson left her more and more confident in her abilities, and more and more confident in the messages she received and transcribed, such that she became a confident, faithful, invincible beacon, never again to doubt the messages she received and transcribed, and never again to doubt her abilities to receive and transcribe them. This woman is you, Angela.

Angela: I can't see how having your confidence shattered can make you more and more confident.

God: *It can, Angela, because it makes you more determined to get it right. It makes you remember the lesson to be sure to quiet your mind. It makes you better at it, and your confidence grows from knowing your abilities have improved because of these lessons.*

Angela: Ok, God, I believe you.

God: *Angela, we don't want to overtax your new-found confidence. So you should go now, and enjoy your evening. But remember that love is the key to success in all things.*

Think love and you cannot fail. Have faith and think love and you are invincible. You are my confident, faithful, invincible beacon.

Creating Your Reality

During her transcription lessons, Angela became well aware of the power of her mind, both to insert information and to create the outcome she desired. She wondered whether the human mind was created that way, or whether it had evolved like that. She asked God about it.

> God: *The human mind was created to be creative. It is therefore necessary to have a fertile imagination, and be able to create thought where before there was none. But also the human mind has evolved, with each person's thoughts adding to the way that the mind works. You know you create your own reality, so if you want to create your mind as a source of only real facts, you can do that. But you also know ultimate reality is the only reality that is real. So love, which is what ultimate reality ultimately is, is the only thing that is real. So keeping your mind focused on love keeps you closer to ultimate reality, as Jesus has taught you earlier.*

Angela had used her creative mind to create the book she thought would help others to learn the lessons which she had learned—hopefully without all the pain. It was nearly finished, when God told her it was time to send her book submission off to the publisher. She hurriedly completed her submission, and sent it off to the publisher she had in mind all along. Angela anxiously awaited a phone call with an offer, but when she saw a letter from the publisher in her mailbox, she knew the outcome was not good.

After receiving her rejection letter, Angela was devastated, and she blamed God. Bill was supportive, which was good, because Angela felt she could no longer put her trust in her spiritual helpers.

When she spoke to Jesus, he consoled her. He told her she had created this situation with her negative thoughts. Eventually, she started to believe him.

Angela: Hello God.

God: *Hello, Angela. You're still talking to me then?*

Angela: Yes, God.

God: *You think I let you down?*

Angela: Well, I did. I don't think that now. What do you think?

God: *You think I let you down, but you and others are creating your own reality. Just like the camel who had to take a wander, sometimes people with free will do things that aren't in keeping with your desires, but remember the aim to cherish every moment, for every moment holds lessons, and every moment holds love.*

Angela: You should have been a politician. You didn't answer the question. Do you think you let me down?

God: *No, Angela, I don't.*

Angela: So, when you said you would never let me down, you meant as long as others don't affect the outcome.

God: *Angela, you know there are no guarantees in life, but I will never let you down. If you ask me, God, for something, it will be yours, as surely as night follows day. But there are no guarantees.*

Angela: Would you like to explain that?

God: *It is as I have told you before. Whatever you desire must come to you. It is the law. But I cannot, and will not, affect any being's free will. So the universe must find a way to bring you your desires, and those of every other being as well.*

Angela: So, God, the universe brings us our desires, and I, and those involved, create our own realities. So, what do you do to ensure you won't let me down?

God: *I love you, Angela. I love you constantly, unconditionally. I love every fibre of your being, every hair on your head, every foible, every wart, everything about you, every cell within you. My love parts seas, Angela. My love creates worlds. My love is you.*

Never fear, for love is here, always. Love is all there is, and I am that. I am the universe that brings you your desires. I am the other person who helps create your reality, and I am you. What do I do, Angela? I do everything. I am everything.

Angela: For some reason, God, that little speech has left me feeling a lot better.

God: *That's good, Angela. Remember, love is all there is. I am all there is. We are one, you and I, and we are love. Be at peace.*

Tools for Coping

Although Angela was still upset about her rejection letter, she found the lessons she had learned about living in the moment and thinking love helped her cope with her disappointment.

God: *I wanted to talk to you to tell you to keep your chin up. You know you are doing the best you can in the circumstances you find yourself in, so don't judge yourself harshly.*

Angela: Ok, God. I wanted to ask you how come I woke up so happy this morning? That happiness stayed with me all day, as long as I remembered to think love. I was very disappointed, but I still managed to be skipping around the office. So what was it? What changed overnight?

God: *Well, Angela, you had another lesson last night, as you slept. You learned a bit more about patience, and a bit more about loving yourself regardless of what others think, and regardless of what happens in your life. So you woke up happy, because you were reminded that you are a wonderful creative being, and that you can create your own reality. You were reminded that no matter what happens in your life, you have all the tools you need to overcome any difficulties, and the main tools are love and faith. Your love worked well today to keep you happy, your faith less so. If you can remember to think love and have faith consistently, you are truly invincible.*

Angela: I know, God. I have felt invincible from time to time. But I guess it was good enough to be happy, in the circumstances.

God: *Yes, Angela. Your love has seen you through another difficult day, and it can see you through any difficulties you may face. Remember that you are a beacon to yourself, as well as the rest of the world. So you can cause your own faith to increase, as well. Appreciate your abilities, and others will as well. Appreciate others abilities; for what you give out comes back to you.*

God Won't Give up on You

Although Angela appreciated all of her lessons, the ones she loved the most were those in which God allowed her to feel some of the vastness of her love.

Angela: Hello, God.

God: *Hello, Angela. I wanted to talk to you, to tell you how much I love you, again. I know you've heard it before, but I don't want you to forget. I love you, Angela.*

Angela: I know, God. I love you, too.

God: *I know, Angela. I appreciate your love. Angela, you are tired, so I won't keep you, but I wanted to give you another demonstration of my love.*

Angela: Ok, God.

…

God: *Just a short one, Angela, but a strong one, yes?*

Angela: Yes, God.

God: *Would you like a little bit more?*

Angela: Yes please, just a little bit.

…

Angela: No, a bit more than that.

…

Angela: Ok. That woke me up.

God: *It did, didn't it? Angela, you are a joy to me. I love to demonstrate my love to you. I love to feel my love flow through you. I would love to demonstrate my love to all the people of the world, but not many know of my existence, and those who know of my existence never think to ask for a physical demonstration of my love. Your book can educate people about my existence, and about the love that is ready to flow to each and every person on the Earth, if they so wish.*

Angela: Thanks again for the demonstration. I feel wonderful again.

God: *So do I, Angela. Thank you, as well. Angela, you can go now and get your dinner, or I can give you another small demonstration.*

Angela: You'll win every time if it's a contest, God.

God: *I'm a bit sneaky like that.*

…

Angela: Ok, God. Love you.

God: *And I love you, Angela, more than words can say, but also more than you can feel, and you can feel a lot.*

Following the rejection of her book, Angela's faith waned. She was no longer confident she could trust Jesus, God, the universe, or herself.

But as time passed, she began to accept what both Jesus and God had told her: she had attracted the rejection of her book with her negative thoughts. She knew she had been worried about allowing so many people to learn of her conversations with the invisible beings. She resolved to be the confident, faithful, invincible beacon she needed to be.

Angela: Hello, God.

God: *Hello, Angela. I love you, Angela. How was your day?*

Angela: It was great, thanks. Because you were there. I felt your love, and there is no way I could argue with the power of love I felt, God.

God: *That's good, Angela. You took a bit of convincing.*

Angela: Not really, God.

God: *Yes really. You still had doubts, even after time after time of feeling my love.*

Angela: Surely not. Well, I guess I did. A bit.

God: *But you are convinced now, aren't you?*

Angela: God, I hope so!

God: *So do I, Angela. Because you know it brings you such joy when you believe in me.*

Angela: It does, God. There is no way I could doubt your love again, surely, after the series of demonstrations you gave today, culminating in the extended demonstration, and my begging you to stop, so that I could get on with my work.

God: *Yes, Angela. It was amusing for me to see and feel you so overwhelmed with my love that you were begging me to stop. But it is also a good lesson for you: that I will never give up on you, Angela. I will do whatever it takes to give you what you desire. You asked if I could restore your faith, and that is what we achieved together, you and I, and your other helpers.*

Angela: Thank you, God. Thank you, all.

God: *You're welcome, Angela. It was a pleasure to envelope you in love. I can do it now again, if you wish.*

…

Angela: O God!

…

Angela: You have left me speechless again.

God: *Not so, me. I am ready to tell you a story.*

Angela: Ok, God.

God: *Once upon a time, there was a beautiful woman who thought she had lost her faith, but when she found it again, it became stronger than ever, such that she never doubted her faith in God again. She never doubted God's love; she never doubted her abilities to hear God's words, to feel God's love. She never doubted herself or God again. For she realised that we are all one; that she can hear God's messages clearly, because she is part of God, and God is part of her. She knew that love is all there is, and love will always prevail in any situation. She knew God would never let her down. She knew God had created the perfect system to bring her all of her desires, and she dwelt in love and peace and joy forever more.*

Angela: God, that is a wonderful story. I hope it is a true story.

God: *Angela, you know you have free will to be, do, and have whatever you choose, but if what you choose is to be the woman in this story, you just need to will it so, and it will be.*

Angela: I do will it so, God. I will that I am the woman in your story, and that your story is true.

God: *Then so it shall be, Angela.*

Go now and celebrate. Be a beacon of God's love and light forever more.

Angela: Ok, God. I love you. I am forever a beacon of your love and light.

Angela had, indeed, lost her faith, but having found it again, she was intent on keeping it. She found it hard to describe the feeling of losing faith. She felt like the veils that were parted had closed back in again, and she was back on her own again. It was like a fog getting thicker and thicker so that she could no longer see her way. She felt like her light, which shines from within, had dimmed, and was no longer visible.

It was only after hearing God's story and accepting it as

her own, that Angela felt the fog begin to lift, and the veils begin to part again.

Be a Beacon

Angela: My faith has been shaky, Jesus, but not any more. I do have complete and utter faith in the universe to bring me my desires, and I now am consistent in my desire to be a published author.

Jesus: *That's good, Angela, but I sense there are still some doubts.*

Angela: I have no doubts in the messages now, Jesus. My doubts are only in my ability to be that invincible beacon. The messages I have transcribed from God, of love and its effect on me, are so alien to the person that I was, the person who had trouble even hugging a friend. My doubts are just whether I can fill the shoes that I have created for myself with these messages from God.

Jesus: *Angela, I know you think it is a big responsibility, and you have experienced love in many ways since your conversations with God began, many ways which are alien to the old you. But remember the point of this book is to bring more love into the world.*

You are a beacon to yourself, as well, remember. You teach what you learn, and you have been having a lot of in-depth lessons, not only about faith, but about love, as well. You can do it, Angela. You can be that invincible beacon of God's love to all the world, and yourself, as well.

Angela: I can, Jesus. (She says, thinking positive.)

Jesus: *Yes, Angela, you can. That is right. You need to think positive. Have faith in yourself, and remember, if this is your desire, the universe must bring you this as well.*

Angela: Ok, Jesus. I can't fail then.

Jesus: *No, Angela. Once you decide on what you want, you can't fail to achieve that.*

Angela: World peace is my major desire, Jesus.

Jesus: *Along with many others, Angela, and that is one reason you are so committed to complete your book, and to be an invincible beacon. Your book, and the love you find so alien can lead to world peace. Have faith, have love, and all will be well.*

Avoid Violence

After speaking to Jesus, Angela spoke to God.

God: *Angela, I wanted to talk to you about last night, and the movie that you left to come and make love with me. I had to remind you of your claim that if there was a contest, I would win every time.*

Angela: Yes, God. That worked.

God: *I noticed. But you were asking why you didn't wake up with the same euphoria to spread through your day. I wanted to let you know that the reason was the movie you were watching, along with the earlier program. The negative images in, particularly the movie—the violence and killing—left residual negativity with you, Angela.*

I know it was only a story, but it still has negativity attached to it. Those images which you placed in your brain dampened down the love we made later. If you recall, you still had some of those images from the movie in your mind, after our love making.

Angela: Yes, God.

God: *So the answer then, Angela, to your question this morning, as to why you didn't wake up with the same feeling of love is, unfortunately, the images you slept with weren't images of love. It is best to avoid any violence, in movies, in sports, in life, if you wish to only experience love.*

Angela: But God, I was told love would always prevail.

God: *Yes, Angela, but only if you continue to think love. Unfortunately, with violent images flashing in your brain, you are not always thinking love.*

Angela: So, we should only enjoy violent movies if we can erase them from our minds?

God: *That's right, Angela, and that is something that is not physically possible. Once it's in there, it's in there for good, or for bad, as the case may be. There is no erase button on your mind. Some memories will fade, but they are always still there, if only a little fainter. So the only way to keep violence out of your mind is to keep violence out of your mind. That is, don't watch it. Don't participate in it.*

As Angela reread those words some weeks later, she remembered the movie she started to watch on TV just the night before.

God spoke to her about it that evening.

God: *Angela, I wanted to talk to you about what you were reading today about violent movies having an effect on your ability to think love, because of the negative images that remain in your mind. By coincidence, which you know does not exist, you just happened to watch another somewhat violent movie last night. You had the good sense to ask for the affects of your mistakes to be removed in all directions of time, as you learned from the fairies, and that worked well. But you know, those images are still there, as you found out this afternoon when one popped into your mind. You did ask, after the movie, for all negative effects of those images to be removed from you, and that has happened, but the fact remains that whilst you are seeing images of violence, it is impossible to think love at the same time. Far better to watch a good comedy, and get some of that best medicine.*

Angela: God, I wondered about those people who have suffered violence against them or have participated in it. There are a lot of people who have not watched a violent movie, but watched a violent life. Will they have trouble moving towards the New Spirituality, because they will have difficulty putting those images out of their minds?

God: *Yes, Angela, they will have difficulty, but as with all things, this problem can be overcome with love. Angela, if enough love is focused on this situation, this problem will also be overcome. Angela, you know love prevails over fear and over violence. It may be hard for those who have participated in violence or had violence inflicted on them to be thinking love all of the time, but if you and the rest of the world can think love in relation to those people, then your love will start to override their fear, and override their violent thoughts. This is why your loving the world is important.*

Once people who have experienced violence start to think love a little, that love will grow within them. You know that like attracts like, and love attracts love, so a few thoughts of love will lead to more thoughts of love, and soon these people, too, will be thinking more love than fear and violence. Love can, indeed, rule the world.

The next day, after loving the world, Angela spoke to God again.

Angela: Hello, God.

God: *Hello, Angela. How was your day?*

Angela: It was better, God. I did remember to think love more, but still not as often as I could have.

God: *No, Angela. You are learning of the benefits. It does help, does it not?*

Angela: Yes, God. It does. Sometimes I wonder if I just become happier because I am amused by the fact that such a silly little thing as thinking love can make such a difference.

God: *It is a little word, but it isn't a silly little thing. Love is a wonderful, marvelous, gorgeous, grand, stupendous, big thing, and thinking of it can only make you feel better.*

Depression

Angela was told love could help her cope with any challenges in life. Unfortunately, the day after Christmas, Boxing Day, brought new challenges to apply these lessons.

Bill woke up in a depressed state. Something Angela said during their morning walk made it worse, and he spent the rest of the day lying on the bed, unable to go to his sister's for his family's get-together.

In his depressed state, he had decided that since the court case was over, and their business was picking up, there must be another reason for his depression. He decided it was Angela.

"You've changed so much since you started doing all these weird witchy things. I just can't cope with you like this."

He wasn't aware of half of what had happened to her, but to him, she had become a different person. In his engineer's practical view of the world, Angela no longer made sense to him.

"You're not even upset about my talking about leaving you."

How could she make him understand? It wasn't that she didn't care. She trusted in the universe that everything would work out in the end.

When she first learned of Bill's resistance to her spiritual awakening, she went to bed one night knowing she would have to leave him, and woke up the next morning knowing she must stay. She somehow knew their destiny lay together as they helped each other evolve. Now, however, she wondered if the situation had changed.

After being unable to resolve his perceived differences with Angela, Bill drove off with rubber burning and gravel flying.

She tried his mobile phone, but heard it ringing in the bedroom. There was nothing she could do but wait and hope. Angela spent a long, sleepless night worrying.

The next day Bill came back.

"I don't know what the solution is, but I don't think it is separation," he said.

Angela breathed a sigh of relief.

They had a long talk and decided to see a psychologist and do more fun things together. They thought there may be a way forward if they could meet somewhere in the middle of their differences.

"Why can't you read a novel, instead of all those spiritual books you seem to be obsessed with?"

"I can do that. And you could read one of my spiritual books. What about *The Power of Now*, by Eckhart Tolle[8]?"

"I can read one of your books, but what about the one I gave you for Christmas?" The book Bill gave her, *Happy For No Reason: 7 Steps To Being Happy From The Inside Out*, by Marci Shimoff[26] was still on the table.

"Yeah, I guess that may be of more benefit at the moment."

Angela was so grateful to have Bill back and that he might

be opening his mind slightly to her spiritual beliefs. She hoped love could overcome any difficulties, as she had been told.

"I love you, Bill, so I'm sure we can work things out."

"And I love you."

Bill managed to pull himself out of the whirlpool of depression with the help of Dr Russ Harris's first book, *The Happiness Trap*[27], but Angela worried she might do something to plunge him back in.

Jesus was able to offer help with those concerns.

> Jesus: *Angela, I know that you fear upsetting Bill, in case you cause him to become depressed again, but you can know that Bill is responsible for his own thoughts and feelings. Yes, you can try to help him be happy, but any changes he needs to make are up to him. You cannot change for him, and neither would you want to.*
>
> *Love yourself before sending your love out into the world, and before loving Bill. You can only love someone else from a position of loving yourself first. Love is the answer to all questions and the solution to all problems. Do not fear. Love will prevail. Be at peace.*

Angela and Bill had their appointment with the psychologist. She mapped out a plan of attack on Bill's depression. She suggested they tackle the depression before any relationship issues were addressed, as depression distorts one's view on everything, and is likely to make issues seem more negative than they otherwise might be.

Very gradually, Bill's mood began to lift. His period of newfound happiness was shortlived, however, as new stresses and problems arose in his life, and bouts of depression unfolded. Sometimes, those stresses were caused by confrontation with Angela's weirdness.

Even though some of Angela's spiritual beliefs were still confronting for Bill, she knew Bill was still evolving, alongside her. He just didn't realise it. And he certainly would never admit it. Ever so slowly, he was beginning to accept her just as she is, but he still had a long way to go before he could let go of the old Angela, who no longer existed.

Angela knew faith and love were the keys to a solution for Bill's depression. She could give love to Bill, and have faith love would prevail over Bill's depression, just as it did over all problems, but she knew Jesus was right. In the end, Bill was responsible for his own thoughts and feelings, and it was up to him if he wanted to change.

When Angela later began research into non-medical treatments for psychological conditions, including depression, her research pointed to meditation as one solution, just as Allan and Jesus had instructed her earlier.

She realised all of her lessons were designed to allow her to cope with her own psychological conditions as they arose, but she also knew if she and others applied these lessons, they might be able to avoid psychological ailments, maybe even all ailments, altogether.

The Tools

Angela began to look back on all she had learned.

She learned how to use energy healing to put her body back into a balanced state, and to help her raise her vibration. She learned Jesus is available to help with healing, and that he, along with her angels and spirit guides, is able to provide advice with many challenges which we all face.

Angela now knew she could cherish every event in her life, even the problems. As well as being a source of spiritual lessons, she knew they could well be stepping stones to something miraculous. With this in mind, it was much easier to follow the advice she had received of: "Don't Worry. Be Happy."

It was much easier for her to be happy when she followed the other advice she had received: to meditate regularly, think love often, and live in the moment. She knew during meditation, she could communicate with her higher self, and that her feelings are its voice. She learned that during meditation, she could release the stress she had built up, and if she thought love and lived in the moment, there was nothing to stress about.

Angela began to notice the miracles which happen every

day, and she knew with faith and love, she could be a creator of miracles. But she also knew she could create nothing without God; she was nothing without God.

She could talk with God whenever she wanted to, whenever she needed to. She knew there was now nothing she needed to fear in this life or the next, and God would be with her throughout every day and throughout every life.

She learned that we are all children of God, and as such, she could create her own reality. She knew the keys are love and faith, and with love and faith, she could move mountains. God had told her: "Ask and you shall receive." She just needed to have faith in her creative abilities and in the universe's abilities to bring her her desires.

Angela also knew if she asked: "What would love do now?" before making any decisions, she would make the right choice. She knew her aim was to think love, to be love, and to act with love in all she did.

Angela learned to avoid violence in any form, so she was happy to avoid violent movies and watch comedies instead. She knew laughter really is the best medicine, so, as well as making her happy, it also made her healthier.

She learned by releasing the joy in another, she could release joy in herself. She knew joy meant that her higher self was pleased with what she was doing.

She knew she could send her peace, love, healing, and joy out into the world and they would be returned tenfold.

Angela: Hello, God. Did you want me to know something?

God: *Yes, Angela, you can know your love is reaching all of its targets. Do not fear. Have faith in yourself, and your abilities. You are my child—a child of God, as is all of my creation. You have the ability to create the reality you desire. Have faith in your creative abilities. You can create your life the way you wish. Others in the world have the same abilities. If you all desire a peaceful world, then that will be your creation.*

Angela: Surely, that is what everyone has always desired.

God: *You would be surprised, Angela, to learn some have welcomed war and conflict as a means to an end. Use love as the means, and love will also be the end.*

The Love Story Continues

Angela knew she was given all the tools she needed to achieve her aim of world peace. She just had to be the confident, faithful, invincible beacon she promised to be. God gave her a lot of other information to help her and those like her to bring about a world where such an outcome was not only possible, but likely.

God told her about the New Spirituality coming to the world, where all the people and creatures of the world would be treated with respect, along with Mother Earth herself. He told Angela that the reason this was possible was because we are all one. We are all God experiencing being human, and we are all humans experiencing being God, and God is love. We are love. All of God's creation is love. And love will prevail—over fear, over disease, over hatred, over everything.

God told her that in the New Spirituality, everyone will understand that we are all instruments of the divine. It matters not whether we believe in God or not; if we are thinking with love, we are thinking as God; if we are acting with love, we are acting as God; and if we are speaking with love, we are speaking the word of God. Angela learned that the word of God was not found in any one religion, but in all religions. All books could be seen as religious texts, and all people seen as God's spiritual teachers. All religions will come to understand that we are one: one God, one people, one creation.

Angela also knew that just as all she had learned could help lead to a reconciliation between all religions and all people of the Earth, it could also bring reconciliation to her relationship with Bill. Just as love could lead to world peace, love could lead to peace in her home. She just had to apply the lessons she learned, of faith and love.

Angela had come a long way since she started her journey. She was now certainly getting used to weird. Getting used to love was taking longer.

She stopped throwing stones from the well-trodden path at those on a new road, and she set about creating a new road for herself. She would be that confident, faithful, invincible beacon she had promised to be. She would shine her light upon her path to God—not so people would follow, but so they would know they could create their own unique path to God and all be beacons for each other. Everyone would know we are all connected by God's love. Everyone would see:

WE ARE ONE.

Look out for the next book from Lorelle Taylor: *We Are One*, which leads Angela through more conversations with God. Find out God's perspective on the major religions, and learn what life will be like in the New Spirituality, when love rules and peace reigns.

Bibliography

1. *A HEALING INITIATION: Rocognize the Healer Within*, Melissa Hocking. Brolga Publishing, Melbourne, 2006.

2. *ASK YOUR ANGELS: A Practical Guide to Working with the Messengers of Heaven to Empower and Enrich Your Life*, Alma Daniel, Timothy Wyllie and Andrew Ramer. Ballantine Books, New York, 1992.

3. *DEVELOPING YOUR OWN PSYCHIC POWERS*, Six CD Set by John Edward. Princess Books, Hay House, Carlsbad, California, 2000.

4. *AFTER LIFE: Answers from the Other Side*, John Edward. Princess Books, New York, 2003.

5. *ASK YOUR GUIDES: Connecting to Your Divine Support System*, Sonia Choquette. Hay House, Carlsbad, California, 2006.

6. www.meditation.org.au

7. *ANGEL MESSAGES FROM THE BEYOND: The Complete Book of Answers*, Juan Nakamori, translated by

Akiko Fujinami published by Rider. Reproduced by permission of The Random House Group Ltd. © 2006

8. *THE POWER OF NOW: A Guide to Spiritual Enlightenment*, Eckhart Tolle. Hachette Australia, Sydney, 2004.

9. *I AM WITH YOU ALWAYS: True Stories of Encounters with Jesus*, G. Scott Sparrow, Ed.D. BCA, London, 1995.

10. *YOU CAN HEAL YOUR LIFE*, Louise Hay. Hay House, Carlsbad, California, 1999.

11. *EXCUSE ME, YOUR GOD IS WAITING: Love Your God * Create Your Life * Find Your True Self*, Michelle Epiphany Prosser. Hampton Roads Publishing, Charlottesville, VA, 2008.

12. Abraham-Hicks, © by Jerry & Esther Hicks, www.abraham-hicks.com, Ph: (830) 755-2299

13. *HOW TO KNOW GOD: The Soul's Journey Into the Mystery of Mysteries*, Deepak Chopra, MD. Three Rivers Press, New York, 2000.

14. *CONVERSATIONS WITH GOD: An Uncommon Dialogue, BOOK 2*, Neale Donald Walsch. Material excerpted from the book *Conversations with God, Book 2* © 1997 By Neale Donald Walsch, used with permission from Hampton Roads Publishing c/o Red Wheel Weiser, LLC Newburyport, MA.

www.redwheelweiser.com, and Hodder and Stoughton, London.

15. *CONVERSATIONS WITH GOD: An Uncommon Dialogue, BOOK 1*, Neale Donald Walsch. Excerpts from CONVERSATIONS WITH GOD: AN UNCOMMON DIALOGUE, BOOK 1 by Neale Donald Walsch, copyright © 1999 by Neale Donald Walsch. Used by permission of TarcherPerigee, an imprint of the Penguin Publishing Group, a division of Penguin Random House LLC, and Hodder and Stoughton, London. All rights reserved.

16. *CONVERSATIONS WITH GOD: An Uncommon Dialogue, BOOK 3*, Neale Donald Walsch. Material excerpted from the book *Conversations with God, Book 3* © 1998 By Neale Donald Walsch, used with permission from Hampton Roads Publishing c/o Red Wheel Weiser, LLC Newburyport, MA. www.redwheelweiser.com, and Hodder and Stoughton, London.

17. *DIET FOR A NEW AMERICA: How Your Food Choices Affect Your Health, Happiness, and the Future of Life on Earth*, John Robbins. HJ Kramer, Tiburon, California & New World Library, Novato, California, 1987.

18. *HEALING WITH THE FAIRIES: Messages, Manifestations, and Love from the World of the Fairies*, Doreen Virtue, Ph.D, © 2001, Hay House, Inc., Carlsbad, California.

19. *FRIENDSHIP WITH GOD: An Uncommon Dialogue*, Neale Donald Walsch. Excerpts from FRIENDSHIP WITH GOD: AN UNCOMMON DIALOGUE by Neale Donald Walsch, copyright © 1999 by Neale Donald Walsch. Used by permission of TarcherPerigee, an imprint of the Penguin Publishing Group, a division of Penguin Random House LLC, and Hodder and Stoughton, London. All rights reserved.

20. "My Love", Written by Tony Hatch. © Universal/MCA Music Publishing Pty Ltd. All rights reserved. International copyright secured. Reprinted with permission.

21. *HOME WITH GOD: In a Life That Never Ends*, Neale Donald Walsch. Excerpts from HOME WITH GOD by Neale Donald Walsch. Copyright © 2006 by Neale Donald Walsch. Reprinted with the permission of Atria Books, a division of Simon & Schuster, Inc, and Hodder and Stoughton, London. All rights reserved.

22. *TOMORROW'S GOD: Our Greatest Spiritual Challenge*, Neale Donald Walsch. Atria Books, New York. 2004.

23. *THE LIGHTWORKER'S WAY: Awakening Your Spiritual Power to Know and Heal*, Doreen Virtue, Ph.D. Hay House, Carlsbad, California. 1997.

24. 4 Corners (ABC), BBC Conspiracy Files: 7/7 https://www.youtube.com/watch?v=rNil0xEcrcY

25. *THE CONFIDENCE GAP: From Fear to Freedom*, Dr Russ Harris, MD. Penguin Group, Camberwell, Victoria. 2010.

26. *HAPPY FOR NO REASON: 7 Steps To Being Happy From The Inside Out*, Marci Shimoff. Simon & Schuster UK Ltd, London. 2008.

27. *THE HAPPINESS TRAP: Stop Struggling, Start Living*, Dr Russ Harris, MD. Exisle Publishing, Wollombi, NSW, 2007.

Recommended Reading

THE SIMPLEST BOOK GOD EVER WROTE, Sunirmalya Symons. Heart Garden Publishing, Deepwater, Qld, 2007.

A RETURN TO LOVE: Reflections on the Principles of "A Course in Miracles", Marianne Williamson. Harper Collins, New York, 1992.

QUANTUM TOUCH: The Power to Heal, Richard Gordon. North Atlantic Books, Berkeley, California, 2006.

Did you enjoy this book?

If you feel like you gained anything from reading this book, others might too. Honest reviews of my book will help others to hear about it. I would be very grateful if you could leave a review at the book retailer of your choice.

Would you like to learn more?

If you would like to hear news from me, including when my next book is released and regular messages from the angels, why not sign up for my mailing list? –
https://www.lorelletaylor.com/subscribe/

If you would like to read my archived blogs, including messages from angels and God, you can search my Blog page –
https://www.lorelletaylor.com/blog/

If you would like to sign up to receive my weekly Card Reading –
https://www.lorelletaylor.com/card-readings/

If you would like to connect with me on Facebook, including seeing my regular angel card readings, and blog posts –
https://www.facebook.com/LorelleKTaylor/

If you would like to connect with me on Instagram for my daily angel card readings –
https://www.instagram.com/lorelle_taylor/

Acknowledgments

There are many beings who have contributed to bringing you this book, and I am unable to thank them all by name.

I must first thank God for all that I am and all that I am yet to be.

Thank you, too, to my spiritual helpers who continue to keep me on the path I chose when I incarnated, and provide me with assistance every day.

This book would not have been possible without the many, many books which came before. As well as those mentioned in this book, there have been many books which have helped to bring me to the place I stand today. Thank you to the many authors and teachers who have contributed to my spiritual education.

Thank you to all of my family, who continue to love me (I think), regardless of my being weird.

Thank you to my friends, particularly those in my New Spirituality Study Group, who have been a great support to me.

Thank you to my editor, Lauren Elise Daniels, who gave me encouragement when I really needed it, and helped to create a book I could be proud of.

Thank you to Jelena (Zelena) from 99designs, who created a beautiful cover for me.

Thank you to all the team at SPF for helping me to go from a writer to a published author.

And last, but not least, I would like to thank you, my reader, for spreading your love and light out into the world and helping to create the world of my dreams—a world where peace reigns and love rules and everyone is treated with respect.

www.ingramcontent.com/pod-product-compliance
Lightning Source LLC
Chambersburg PA
CBHW032037290426
44110CB00012B/842